Terrific

TOM SEAVER | 1944–2020

DAILY NEWS

TRIUMPH BOOKS

Copyright © 2020 by The New York Daily News

No part of this publication may be reproduced, stored in a retrieval system or transmitted in any form by any means, electronic, mechanical, photocopying or otherwise, without prior written permission of the publisher, Triumph Books LLC, 814 North Franklin Street; Chicago, Illinois 60610.

Library of Congress Publication-in-Catalog Data available upon request

This book is available in quantity at special discounts for your group or organization.
For further information, contact:

Triumph Books LLC
814 North Franklin Street
Chicago, Illinois 60610
Phone: (312) 337-0747
www.triumphbooks.com

Printed in U.S.A.
ISBN: 978-1-62937-896-1
Design and page production by Patricia Frey
Cover design by Preston Pisellini

This is an unofficial publication. This book is in no way affiliated with, licensed by, or endorsed by Major League Baseball, the New York Mets, the Seaver family, or any associated entities.

Contents

Tom Seaver, the Greatest Met of All Time, Dies at 75
by Bill Madden 4

Mets, Baseball React to Tom Seaver's Death
by Deesha Thosar 33

"It Was an Honor to Watch Him Pitch" *by Kerry Burke* 45

Johnny Bench Remembers His Friend and Teammate
Tom Seaver *by Bill Madden* 52

Tom Seaver, the First One Who Made Mets Fans
Believe, Was the Ace of New York *by Mike Lupica* 60

Remembering Tom Seaver, the Broadcaster
by Bob Raissman 68

Memories of Tom Terrific: How the Legend Gave
a Chance to a Rookie Writer *by Malka Drucker* 77

When God Was a Mets Fan: How the Miracle in '69
Happened *by Jacqueline Cutler* 83

Seaver to Reds and King to Padres *by Jack Lang* 90

An Old Friend Comes Home and Thrills Us
by Mike Lupica 97

Tom Terrific's Decorated Major League Journey Began
53 Years Ago Today *by Deesha Thosar* 105

Seaver's Retirement Bittersweet *by Jack Lang* 110

Cheers Hug Seaver *by Bill Madden* 117

Tom Seaver's Friends Cherish a Lifetime of Memories
with the Greatest Met *by Bill Madden* 125

Wednesday, September 2, 2020

TOM SEAVER, THE GREATEST MET OF ALL TIME, DIES AT 75

by Bill Madden

The long goodbye has ended. The Mets' "Franchise" is gone.

Tom Seaver, the greatest of all Mets who dropped out of public life in March of 2019 after being diagnosed with dementia died early Monday. According to family sources, Seaver, 75, died peacefully at his home in Calistoga, Calif., from complications from Lyme disease, dementia and COVID-19.

He leaves behind 311 victories, 3,640 career strikeouts, three Cy Young Awards and countless millions New York baseball fans who forever cherish the memories of the Miracle Mets 1969 championship season and his starring role in it.

"We are heartbroken to share that our beloved husband and father has passed away," said his wife Nancy Seaver and daughters Sarah and Anne in a statement to the Baseball Hall of Fame. "We send our love out to his fans, as we mourn his loss with you."

In the annals of baseball there will never be a more improbable World Series champion than the '69 Mets, who had never had a winning season since their inception in 1962. Seaver was the catalyst, the ace of a young and talented pitching staff that included Jerry Koosman, Nolan Ryan and Gary Gentry, who all blossomed together. Leading the league with 25 wins en route to his first Cy Young

TOM SEAVER | 1944–2020

New York Mets pitcher Tom Seaver poses for a photo in March 1968. (AP Photo)

TOM SEAVER | 1944–2020

Award, Seaver hurled eight consecutive complete game victories from Aug. 31-Sept. 27 as the Mets rallied from as far back as 10 games behind on Aug. 13 to chase down Leo Durocher's Cubs. The pivotal series which broke the slumping Cubs' back was Sept. 8-9 at Shea Stadium in which Koosman out-pitched Chicago's Bill Hands, 3-2 with a 13-strikeout effort in the first game, and Seaver, backed by homers from Donn Clendenon and Art Shamsky, triumphed over fellow future Hall of Famer, Ferguson Jenkins, in the second game to bring the Mets to within one-half game of first place. They went into first place by sweeping a doubleheader from the Expos the next night and never relinquished it.

Earlier that season, on July 9 against the Cubs, Seaver pitched what he called the "greatest game of my career" in an emotionally-charged night at Shea when he took a perfect game into the ninth inning only to lose it on a one-out looping single to left-center field by unsung reserve outfielder Jimmy Qualls. Seaver took two other no-hitters into the ninth inning in his career before finally succeeding, June 16, 1978, against the Cardinals while a member of the Reds.

"A no-hitter is momentary," he said afterward. "You enjoy the moment. But nothing can ever compare to winning a World Series."

After sweeping the Atlanta Braves, 3-0, in the '69 National League Championship Series, the Mets completed their miracle season by upsetting the Orioles of Frank and Brooks Robinson, Jim Palmer and Boog Powell, who'd led the majors with 109 wins, in the World Series. After giving up a game-opening homer to the Orioles' Don Buford, Seaver was out-pitched by Mike Cuellar in Game 1, but redeemed himself mightily by holding the Orioles to one run in a 10-inning complete game victory in Game 4. The next day, Koosman hurled another complete game to clinch the Series.

It was sometime during the '69 season that Jack Lang, the Mets beat writer for the *Long Island Press*, began referring to Seaver as "Tom Terrific" in his game stories — a moniker that stuck for the rest of his career and beyond.

But there was so much more to the Seaver lore beyond the '69 championship season, beginning in 1966 when he became an accidental Met. After growing up in Fresno, Calif., and graduating from high school, he got no college scholarship offers because he was too small. Instead, he decided to enroll in the Marine Corps reserves whereupon, in six months, he grew from 5-9, 160-pounds to 6-1, 210. Suddenly, he was a prospect, and in 1965 earned a scholarship to USC under the legendary coach Rod Dedeaux, and was 10-2 with 100 strikeouts in 100 innings.

Rookie pitchers Tom Seaver (left) and Bill Denehy of the Mets trot around Shea Stadium in 1967. (Charles Payne/NY Daily News Archive)

Tom Seaver pitching against the Pittsburgh Pirates in 1967. (Frank Hurley/NY Daily News Archive)

> *Seaver set a slew of strikeout records. On April 22, 1970, he tied the major league record by striking out 19 San Diego Padres in one game, including another record 10 strikeouts in a row to finish it.*

The following January he was drafted by the Braves, the favorite team of his youth because of Hank Aaron, whom he idolized. But after agreeing to a contract for $40,000, plus an additional $11,500 to complete his college education, Seaver suddenly found himself in no-man's land. It seemed USC had already begun their new season when Seaver signed the contract, a violation of major league rules. Thus, the contract had to be voided, but at the same time, Seaver was now also ineligible to return to school. After his father, Charles, a world class amateur golfer who was a member of the 1932 Walker Cup team, threatened to sue baseball, Commissioner William Eckert resolved the issue by setting up a lottery in which any teams willing to match the Braves' offer could participate for Seaver's services. Only three teams, the Indians, Phillies and Mets, stepped forward and Eckert picked the Mets out of a hat.

Seaver spent only one year of minor league apprenticeship, earning a spot in the Mets rotation in 1967 where he proceeded to win National League Rookie of the Year honors with a 16-13 record and 2.76 ERA. When Gil Hodges took over as Mets manager in 1968, Seaver called it a transformational event in his career. He immediately bonded with the former standout Dodger first baseman and ex-Marine, and later said Hodges was the most influential person in his life after his father.

If there was one thing Seaver made clear when he joined the Mets it was that he wanted nothing to do with the "lovable losers" image they'd acquired ever since setting the major league record of 120 losses in 1962. When he beat the Dodgers, 5-2, June 3, 1969, to lift the Mets over .500 for the first time in their history, he seethed at a reporter's question about it being worthy of a champagne celebration. "Champagne?" he snapped. "Five-hundred is nothing to celebrate. It's mediocrity. Maybe Marv Throneberry and Rod Kanehl (two of the legendary inept '62 Mets) will celebrate. But I had nothing to do with that. The only time for champagne is when we win a World Series."

Beginning in 1968, Seaver set a slew of strikeout records. On April 22, 1970, he tied the major league record by striking out 19 San

TOM SEAVER | 1944–2020

Tom Seaver with Mets right-hander Nolan Ryan. (NY Daily News Archive)

Hallucinating —By Bill Gallo

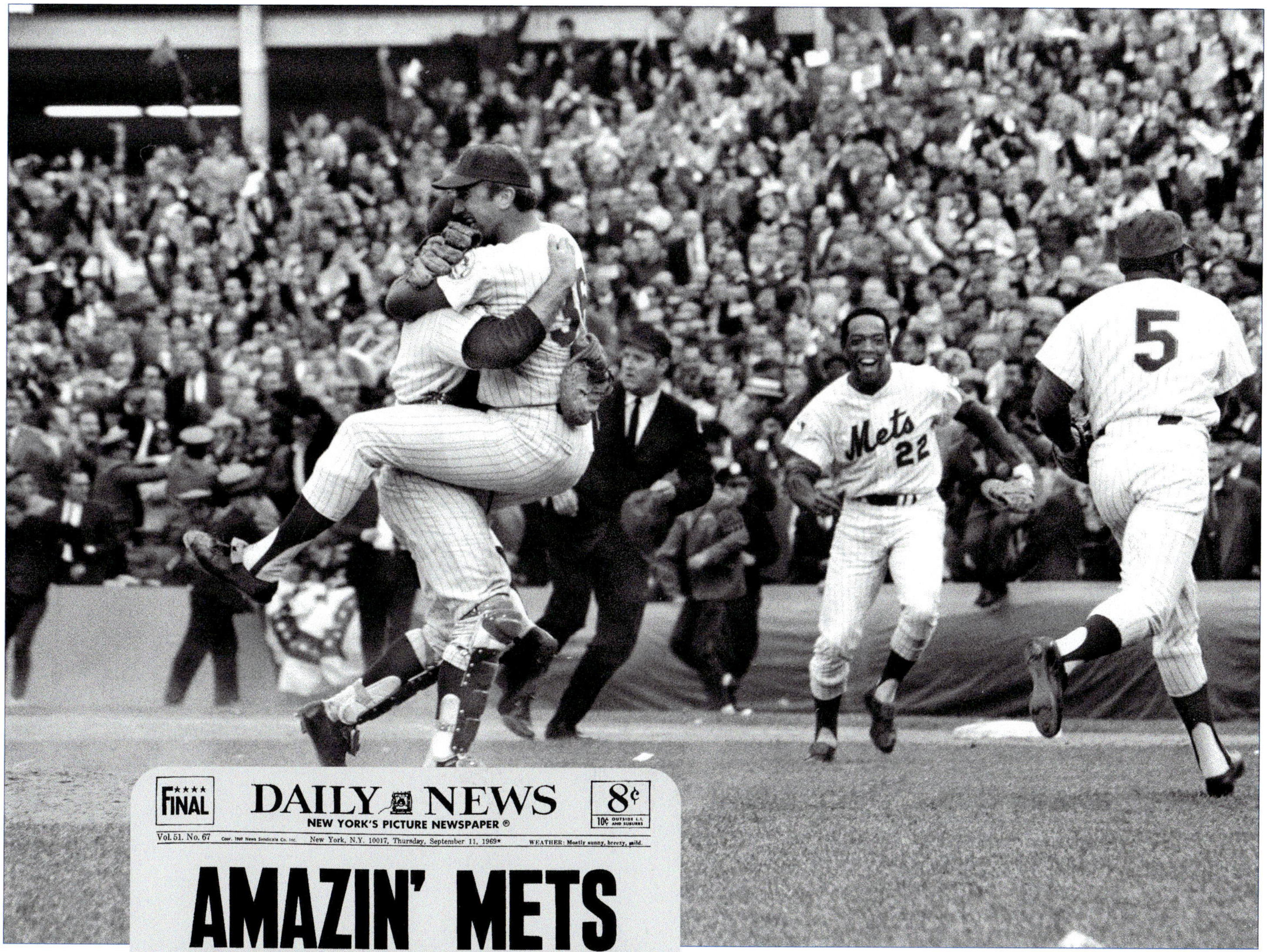

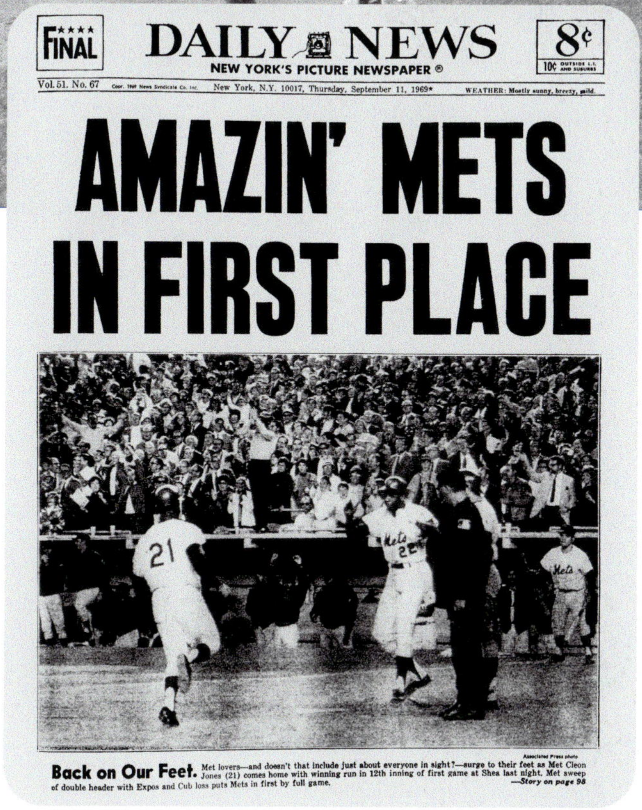

FINAL ★★★★ | DAILY NEWS | 8¢

NEW YORK'S PICTURE NEWSPAPER ®

10¢ OUTSIDE L.I. AND SUBURBS

Vol. 51. No. 67 Copr. 1969 News Syndicate Co. Inc. New York, N.Y. 10017, Thursday, September 11, 1969* WEATHER: Mostly sunny, breezy, mild.

AMAZIN' METS IN FIRST PLACE

Associated Press photo

Back on Our Feet. Met lovers—and doesn't that include just about everyone in sight?—surge to their feet as Met Cleon Jones (21) comes home with winning run in 12th inning of first game at Shea last night. Met sweep of double header with Expos and Cub loss puts Mets in first by full game. —*Story on page 98*

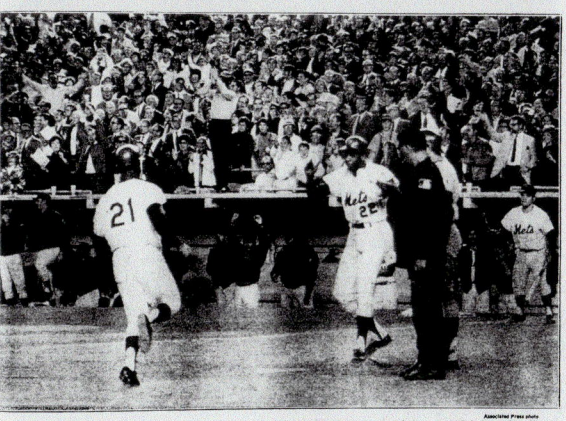

(Facing page) June 21, 1969. Hallucinating, Pennant (Bill Gallo/NY Daily News Archive); (Top) Mets winning pitcher Jerry Koosman jumps into the arms of Jerry Grote after the Mets defeated the Baltimore Orioles 5-3 in Game 5 of the 1969 World Series. (Paul DeMaria/NY Daily News Archive); (Left) Daily News *front page, September 11, 1969. (NY Daily News Archive)*

Mets manager Gil Hodges sports a smile with Jerry Koosman, Tom Seaver, and Nolan Ryan, at Shea Stadium. (Gene Kappock/NY Daily News Archive)

Diego Padres in one game, including another record 10 strikeouts in a row to finish it. From 1968-76, he set the all-time record of nine consecutive 200-strikeout seasons. His career total of 3,640 ranks sixth on the all-time list; his 61 shutouts tied for seventh with Ryan.

In 1970 and '71, Seaver led the NL in both ERA (2.81 and 1.76) and strikeouts (283 and 289) but did not win the Cy Young Award. It wasn't until 1973, when he led the Mets to their second World Series, with a 19-10 record and league leading 2.08 ERA, 18 complete games, 251 strikeouts and 0.976 WHIP, that he became the first pitcher to win the Cy Young without winning 20 games. He won his third and final Cy Young in 1975, leading the NL in wins (22-9) and strikeouts (243). But the following year, with the dawning of free agency in baseball, trouble with Mets upper management developed.

As the Mets' union representative, Seaver had worked hard to bring about a new system in baseball eliminating the reserve clause that had essentially bound players to their teams for life, and in that role incurred the enmity of Mets board chairman M. Donald Grant, who at one point during labor negotiations confronted him in the clubhouse and said: "What are you, a Communist?" At the end of the '76 season, the two became embroiled in an increasingly nasty contract dispute, with Grant enlisting the support of the *Daily News*' powerful sports columnist, Dick Young, to write a series of columns highly critical of Seaver. "Tom Tewwific is a pouting, griping, morale-breaking clubhouse lawyer, poisoning the team," Young wrote in launching his offensive.

Despite being highly critical of Grant's refusal to engage in the bidding for any of the premium free agents, Seaver made it clear to Mets owner Lorinda de Roulet he did not want to leave the Mets, and agreed to a three-year contract, with a base salary of $325,000 through 1978. But right before the June 15, 1977, trading deadline, Seaver became enraged with a column by Young that brought his wife, Nancy, into the fray: "Nolan Ryan is getting more now than Seaver, and that galls Tom because Nancy Seaver and Ruth Ryan are very friendly and Tom Seaver has long treated Nolan Ryan like a little brother."

That was it. Seaver called Mets GM Joe McDonald, screaming "get me out of here" and the next day, in what was dubbed the "Midnight Massacre," Grant traded Seaver to the Reds for four players, pitcher Pat Zachry, second baseman Doug Flynn, and outfielders Steve Henderson and Dan Norman. Later that night he traded the Mets top slugger, Dave Kingman, to the Padres for Bobby Valentine.

In the New York newspapers of June 16, Grant and Young were universally pilloried for driving Seaver out of town, none more so than Young's own *Daily News* in which columnist Pete Hamill wrote: "There is, of course, no way to discuss the departure of Tom Seaver without discussing the role of Dick Young. Nothing is more squalid than a quarrel between writers and I have too much respect for Young's talents to want to pick a fight with him. But for almost two years Young has been functioning as a hit man for Mets management and in that role he helped drive a great ballplayer out of town, helped demoralize younger men and worst of all has demeaned his own talents."

Seaver went on to win 75 more games for the Reds from 1977-81, but after a bout with shoulder tendinitis in 1980 landed him on the disabled list for a month for the first time in his career, he was no longer a pure power pitcher. He was, however, still acknowledged as the smartest pitcher in the game. In the 1981 "split season" that was interrupted by a 50-day players strike, he led the NL in wins (14-2) while striking out only 87 batters in 166⅓ innings.

It was ironically the element that ultimately settled the '81 strike (which he helped negotiate) — indirect compensation to teams that lost free agents in the form of a pool of unprotected players — that led to Seaver's second departure from the Mets three years later. Following an injury-plagued 5-13 season in '82, it was agreed by Seaver and the Reds that they should part ways and a trade was worked out that sent him back home to the Mets for a second-line starting pitcher, Charlie Puleo.

It was, however, a terrible (68-94) Mets team Seaver rejoined in '83, and though he was able to log over 200 innings for the first time since '79, he had his second straight (9-14) losing record. Disappointing as that had been, it was nothing compared to the shock he incurred the following January when he was selected by the White Sox out of the free agent compensation pool after the Mets had incomprehensibly left him off their protected list. In taking full blame for the blunder, Mets GM Frank Cashen said he didn't think the White Sox would take a 40-year-old pitcher, especially one like Seaver who was acknowledged to be a New York icon and the Mets' "franchise" player.

Seaver won 15 games in 1984 for the White Sox including two in one day, May 9, when he was called upon to pitch the final inning of an eight-hour game that had been suspended from the night before, and then pitched 8⅓ innings in his own scheduled start. The following year, he won 16 games for the White Sox. None of them were more notable, however, than August 4 against the Yankees when he upstaged Phil Rizzuto on his "day" at Yankee Stadium with his 300th career victory — a six-hit, seven strikeout complete game with the appropriate score of 4-1, his career uniform number.

By then, Seaver had grown homesick and longed to go back to New York so he could spend more time with his wife and two daughters. After first engaging with George Steinbenner to no avail on a trade with the Yankees, White Sox general manager "Hawk" Harrelson was able to satisfy Seaver by sending him to the Red Sox, June 29, 1986, for infielder Steve Lyons. It was an injury-plagued 7-13 '86 season for Seaver, however,

TOM SEAVER | 1944–2020

Tom Seaver and J.C. Martin embrace in the Mets dugout after another victory. (Frank Hurley/NY Daily News Archive)

Terrific | DAILY NEWS

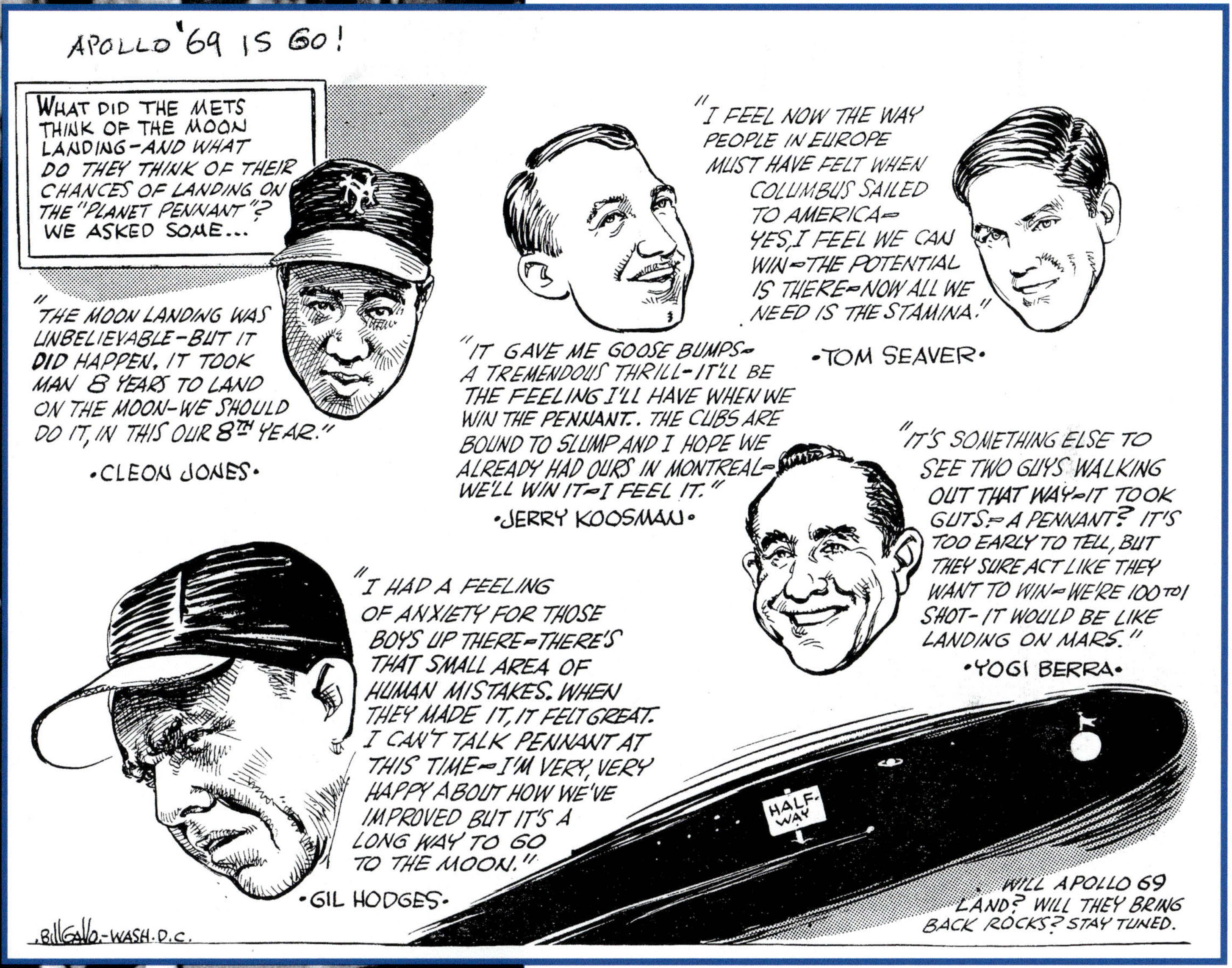

TOM SEAVER | 1944–2020

(Left) Rod Gaspar leaps on home plate and a jacketed Tom Seaver leaps for joy in Game 4 of the 1969 World Series. (Paul DeMaria/NY Daily News Archive); (Above) Apollo '69 is a Go! (Bill Gallo/NY Daily News Archive)

and a knee issue consigned him to being spectator in the World Series against his old team, the Mets, when the Red Sox left him off their postseason roster.

In May of '87, at Cashen's request, Seaver attempted a comeback with the Mets, hoping to end his career where it started, but it was not to be. After spending a couple of weeks trying to work his way back with the Mets' Triple-A Norfolk team, Seaver concluded that he was regressing rather than progressing, and on June 22, 1987, announced his retirement at Shea Stadium. "I would have loved to help this team win another world championship," he said, "but there are no more pitches in this 42-year-old arm. I've used them all up." A year later, the Mets retired his No. 41, and his list of Mets records — wins (198), complete games (171), shutouts (44), starts (395), innings (3,045), strikeouts (2,541) and ERA (2.57) — will likely stand forever.

In his post-playing career Seaver worked as an analyst in the WPIX Yankee broadcast booth from 1989-93 and later did the same with the Mets from 1999-2005. In 1992, he was elected to the Hall of Fame with the highest percentage (98.8%) ever to that time. "There were very few times in my career when I was speechless, but the magnitude that goes with the Hall of Fame and the numbers…I'm at a total disbelief at that percentage," he said.

But as he later told intimates, broadcasting just wasn't satisfying enough for him. He needed a new challenge and, in 1998, he told Nancy he wanted to move from their longtime home in Greenwich, Conn., to California and make wine. He purchased 115 acres of dense brush on the top of Diamond Mountain in Calistoga and created a vineyard where he produced cabernet sauvignon. In 2008, his GTS (for George Thomas Seaver) cabernet was accorded a 97 rating by the Wine Spectator.

Sadly, he was unable to fully enjoy his successful second career and new life as a California winemaker. Sometime around 2010-2011 he began having memory issues, mood swings and occasional flu-like symptoms. Fearing he'd had a stroke or was suffering from Alzheimer's disease, he did nothing about it. It wasn't until one day in 2012 when he couldn't remember the name of his head vineyard worker that Nancy insisted he see a doctor.

In March of 2013 Seaver revealed to the *Daily News* that he was suffering from a recurrence of the Lyme disease, which he first contracted in 1991 working in his garden in Greenwich. Because he had taken so long to get it diagnosed, doctors told him the damage to his brain was irreversible and his memory loss would likely gradually get worse. In October of 2018, he shut off communication with his friends. The following March the Hall of Fame put out a statement that Seaver was suffering from dementia. He is survived by his wife, Nancy, and two daughters, Sarah and Anne.

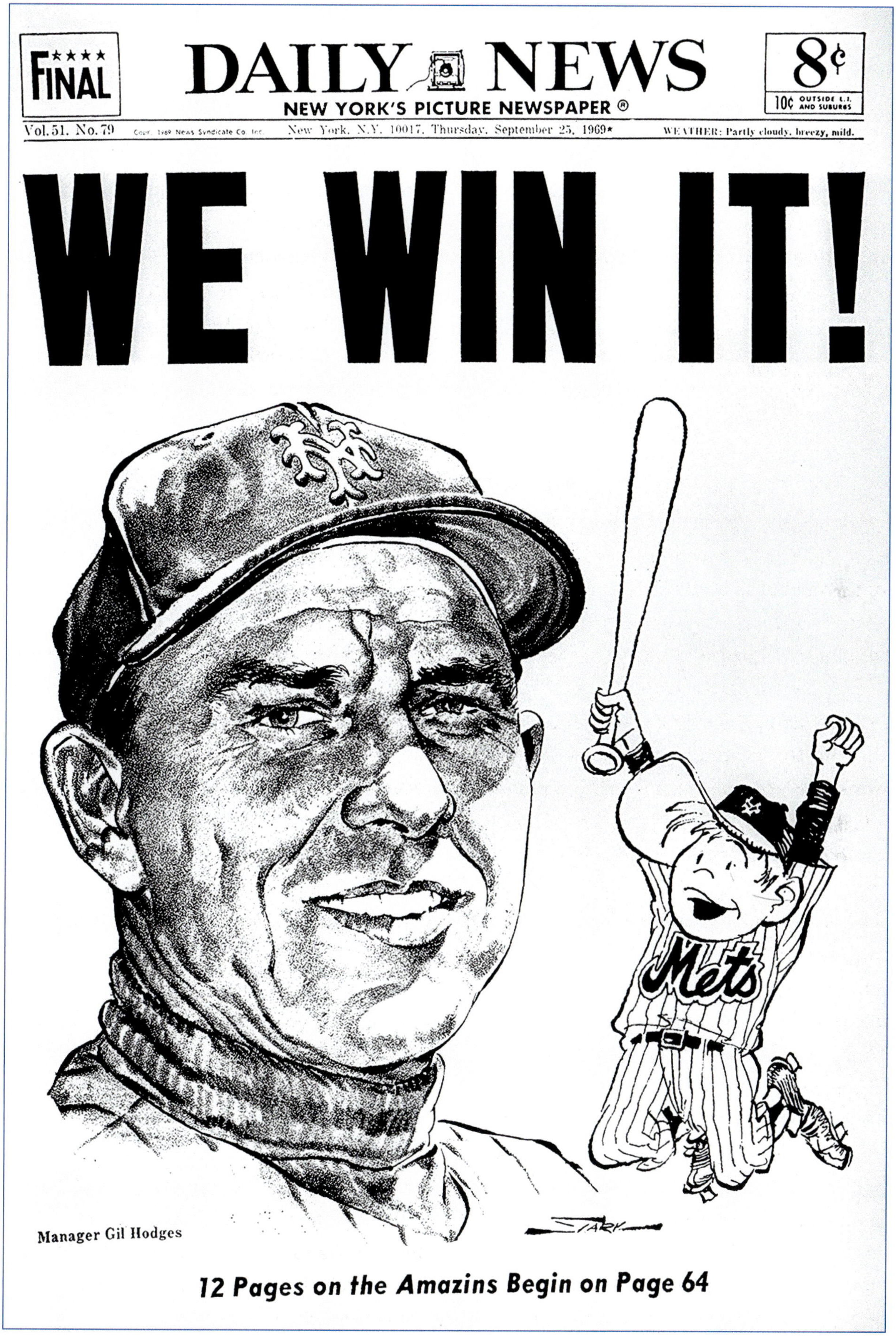

FINAL ★★★★

DAILY NEWS

NEW YORK'S PICTURE NEWSPAPER ®

8¢

10¢ OUTSIDE L.I. AND SUBURBS

Vol. 51. No. 79 Copr. 1969 News Syndicate Co. Inc. New York, N.Y. 10017, Thursday, September 25, 1969★ WEATHER: Partly cloudy, breezy, mild.

WE WIN IT!

Manager Gil Hodges

12 Pages on the Amazins Begin on Page 64

Daily News *front page, September 25, 1969. (NY Daily News Archive)*

(Above) J.C. Martin and Donn Clendenon congratulate Mets pitcher Tom Seaver after a winning performance in Game 4 of the World Series against the Baltimore Orioles. (John Duprey/NY Daily News Archive); (Facing page) Tom Seaver winds up for a pitch in Game 1 of the World Series in 1969. (AP Photo)

TOM SEAVER | 1944–2020

Terrific | DAILY NEWS

(Right) Tom Seaver is head and shoulders above winning pitcher Nolan Ryan after the Mets won the 1969 NL pennant. (Paul Demaria/NY Daily News Archive); (Above) July 17, 1969: "Today the moon – tomorrow the world!" (Bill Gallo/NY Daily News Archive)

TOM SEAVER | 1944–2020

Terrific | DAILY NEWS

TOM SEAVER | 1944–2020

Fans swarm the field at Shea Stadium after the Mets won the World Series. (Ed Clarity/NY Daily News Archive)

TOM SEAVER | 1944–2020

(Facing page) Mets owner Joan Whitney Payson receives special Page One. (James Garrett/NY Daily News Archive); (Top) 1969 Mets team photo (AP Photo)

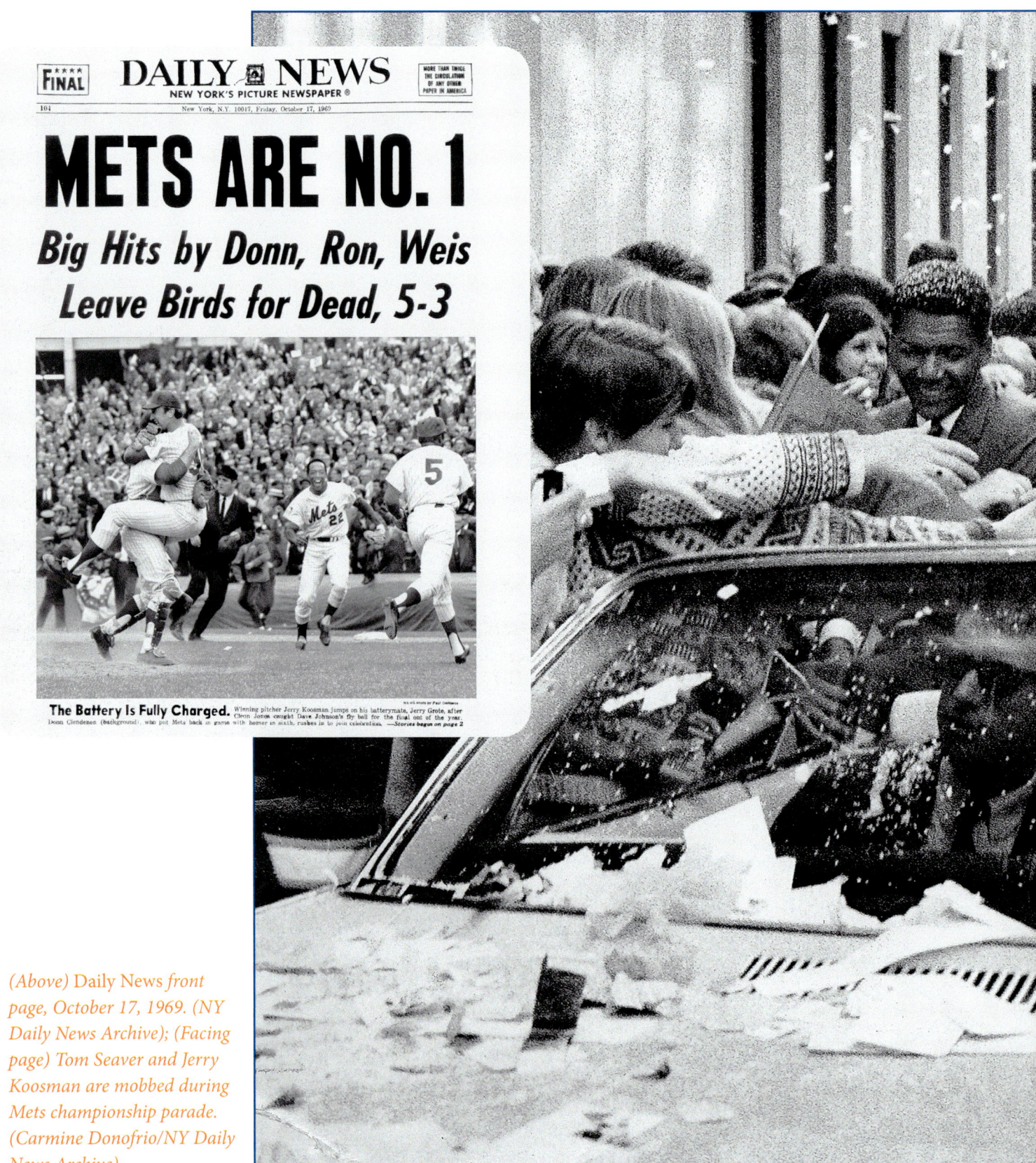

(Above) Daily News *front page, October 17, 1969. (NY Daily News Archive); (Facing page) Tom Seaver and Jerry Koosman are mobbed during Mets championship parade. (Carmine Donofrio/NY Daily News Archive)*

TOM SEAVER | 1944–2020

TOM SEAVER | 1944–2020

Wednesday, September 2, 2020

METS, BASEBALL REACT TO TOM SEAVER'S DEATH

by Deesha Thosar

Tom Seaver was more than a Hall of Famer. To the Mets family, he was more than the greatest pitcher of all time.

Seaver was The Franchise. Seaver was the heart and soul of the organization. Every baseball player, coach, manager or staff member that came after him and was affiliated with the Mets was instantly aware of his legacy.

He peacefully passed away in his Calistoga, Calif. home on Monday at the age of 75 after a battle with dementia, Lyme disease and complications from COVID-19. Seaver retired from public life in March 2019.

Seaver's Mets teammates and later-era Mets greats praised him on Wednesday. "A great leader of our team," fellow starter Jerry Koosman said. "When he wasn't pitching he was always there to help the other guys on the staff."

"He had a great head on his shoulders," Mets mainstay Ed Kranepool said. "We became a different team when he walked into the locker room in 1967."

It wasn't just ex-teammates who loved Seaver. "I'll always treasure our friendship," Mike Piazza said. "Two of my fondest memories are walking out of Shea Stadium together after the last game and then when he threw the ceremonial first pitch to me at Citi Field the next year. He was one of a kind."

Piazza and Seaver are the only two players in Mets caps in the Hall of Fame, something Piazza said mattered to Seaver.

The Mets take a moment of silence in memory of Tom Seaver before a game against the New York Yankees at Citi Field on September 3, 2020. (Sarah Stier/Getty Images)

> *"It's a sad day for me. One of the first calls I got after I won my Cy Young in 1985 was from Tom. That meant the world to me."*
>
> —Dwight Gooden

"It's a sad day for me," Dwight Gooden said. Gooden's career with the Mets began in 1984, the year after Seaver's final season with the team. "One of the first calls I got after I won my Cy Young in 1985 was from Tom. That meant the world to me."

Mets CEO Fred Wilpon and his son, COO Jeff, released a joint statement on the passing of their beloved World Series champion:

"We are devastated to learn of the passing of Mets Legend and Baseball Hall of Famer Tom Seaver. Tom was nicknamed 'The Franchise' and 'Tom Terrific' because of how valuable he truly was to our organization and our loyal fans, as his #41 was the first player number retired by the organization in 1988. He was simply the greatest Mets player of all time and among the best to ever play the game which culminated with his near unanimous induction into the National Baseball Hall of Fame in 1992.

"Beyond the multitude of awards, records, accolades, World Series Championship, All-Star appearances, and just overall brilliance, we will always remember Tom for his passion and devotion to his family, the game of baseball, and his vineyard.

"Our thoughts and prayers go out to his wife, Nancy, daughters Sarah and Anne and four grandsons, Thomas, William, Henry and Tobin."

Keith Hernandez, who played against Seaver before becoming his first baseman for the Mets in 1983, went to Twitter to express his emotions.

"I am deeply saddened of the passing of Tom Seaver," Hernandez tweeted. "I had the honor of unsuccessfully hitting against him & having as a teammate. He is the greatest Met of all time. No one will ever surpass him that wears the orange & blue. My condolences to Nancy & his family. Tears."

Tom Seaver during a game in 1975. (AP Photo/David Durochik)

Tom Seaver's No. 41 jersey hangs in the Mets dugout before the start of a game against the New York Yankees at Citi Field on September 3, 2020. (AP Photo/Kathy Willens)

TOM SEAVER | 1944–2020

Manager Luis Rojas, who has served in the Mets organization for the past 13 years, was distraught upon learning of the sad news.

"Wow, that's tough," said Rojas, seconds after he found out of Seaver's passing. "It's terrible news, especially for the Mets family."

"We all knew that Tom had been suffering the last few years," said SNY broadcaster Gary Cohen. "There's a sadness, but there's also a light there because Tom represented our childhood. He was a light that we could all look to. He was the best at his craft, the leader of his team, he was immaculate in the way he approached his job. He was a good person, he was a tough person.

"He was the one person who changed the entire notion of what it was to be a New York Mets fan."

"Oh everything," Mets broadcaster Howie Rose said of what Seaver meant to him, both as a fan and then later, as a colleague. "I'm no pitching coach or savant, but to these pedestrian eyes he was so technically proficient. I was a young radio reporter in 1977 when he was not long from being traded to Cincinnati. I met him in a postgame scenario ... But later on I would eventually work with him on air from time to time and that was magical."

"He was the smartest pitcher I ever caught," said catcher Duffy Dyer, who caught Seaver from 1968-74.

MLB Commissioner Rob Manfred Jr. also issued a statement on the three-time Cy Young Award winner and 12-time All-Star:

"I am deeply saddened by the death of Tom Seaver, one of the greatest pitchers of all time. Tom was a gentleman who represented the best of our National Pastime. He was synonymous with the New York Mets and their unforgettable 1969 season. After their improbable World Series Championship, Tom became a household name to baseball fans — a responsibility he carried out with distinction throughout his life.

"On behalf of Major League Baseball, I extend my condolences to Tom's family, his admirers throughout our game, Mets fans, and the many people he touched."

Baseball devotees around the nation honored Seaver and what he meant to the sport. He was elected to the Hall of Fame in 1992 after retiring from a 20-year career in 1986.

"Tom Seaver's life exemplified greatness in the game, as well as integrity, character, and sportsmanship — the ideals of a Hall of Fame career," said Jane Forbes Clark, Chairwoman of the National Baseball Hall of Fame and Museum.

Tom Seaver in the Mets clubhouse. (Dan Farrell/NY Daily News Archive)

TOM SEAVER | 1944–2020

TOM SEAVER | 1944–2020

(Facing page) Tom Seaver on the streets of New York. (Anthony Pescatore/NY Daily News Archive); (Above) Tom Seaver and his wife, Nancy, reading the Daily News. *(Dan Farrell/NY Daily News Archive)*

(Above) Tom Seaver and Jerry Grote during the 1969 World Series. (NY Daily News Archive);
(Facing page) Tom Seaver has his throwing form checked. (NY Daily News Archive)

TOM SEAVER | 1944–2020

Wednesday, September 2, 2020

"IT WAS AN HONOR TO WATCH HIM PITCH"

New Yorkers saddened at death of Mets icon Tom Seaver

by Kerry Burke

More than a half-century after Tom Seaver brought a baseball "miracle" to New York, the city still kept him in its heart.

New Yorkers on Wednesday night hailed the Hall of Famer and Mets hero, who died at the age of 75, for leaving a legacy of pride and hope at a time the city needs it the most.

"It epitomizes 2020 — it's another unbelievable loss," Chase Gornbein, 22, of Manhattan, said of the death of "Tom Terrific."

At an outside table at an Upper West Side bar, Gornbein said he was too young to have seen Seaver on the mound, but the "icon" was burned into his memory anyhow.

"Tom Seaver was a childhood hero," he said. "He was one of the people you grew up wanting to be. My father said, 'Be like Tom,' and I wanted that."

The Mets joined the National League in 1962, and were baseball bottom-feeders the first few seasons.

Tom Seaver on the mound for the Mets. (Bettmann / Contributor)

TOM SEAVER | 1944–2020

Michael Leavitt, 23, an Upper West Side financier, said Seaver brought the most precious thing he could to the Mets.

"He brought hope to the Mets when few others could," he said of Seaver, who debuted as a 22-year-old in 1967. "He will always be remembered. Seaver embodied the era of Mets excellence. He will always be remembered for that. You say Seaver, you thought baseball, you thought New York. You definitely thought the Mets."

In 1969, with Seaver going 25-7 and winning the first of his three Cy Young Awards, the "Miracle Mets" stunned baseball by winning the World Series.

Ardent Mets fan Milton Walters, 60, of Brooklyn, a freelance photographer and union carpenter, said his first brush with the baseball giant was during the 1969 Series.

"I was 9 years old and watched him on a 13-inch black and white Zenith television," Walters recalled. "My grandmother was a hard-core Mets fan and made us watch the game. From then on, I was hooked."

When Seaver pitched, Walters marveled, "he dragged his knee on the ground. The Mets were more human."

"Seaver was what he was stated to be, he was The Franchise," he said of one of Seaver's nicknames.

"It was an honor to watch him pitch. He was a craftsman and a flame-thrower. He was my favorite Met."

Tom Seaver in Game 1 of the 1969 World Series. (Dan Farrell/ NY Daily News Archive)

TOM SEAVER | 1944–2020

Michael Jaggers-Radolf, 39, who works in finance in Manhattan, said he'll not soon forget Seaver's remarkable career.

"He was a class act," he said. "Statistically he was the most dominant pitcher ever. When he was an announcer, what a spokesman for baseball! He's an icon."

Jaggers-Radolf lamented, however, that his heart has ached ever since Seaver was diagnosed with dementia.

"The loss already happened," he mourned.

Asher Ripp, 22, a clinical researcher who also lives on the Upper West Side, said Seaver encapsulated baseball excellence.

"Oh my God, he was all-time New York and an all-time Met for sure. Where do you start? He threw no-hitters, and on and on. He even played baseball into '80s. It's a monumental loss for baseball."

(Facing page) Tom Seaver is engulfed by teammates after striking out 19 San Diego Padres. (Dan Farrell/NY Daily News Archive); (Above) Bud Harrelson and Tom Seaver, along with Seaver's wife, Nancy, celebrate Seaver's performance. (Dan Farrell/NY Daily News Archive)

TOM SEAVER | 1944–2020

(Facing page) Bob Scheffing and Tom Seaver are a happy pair after announcing deal that makes Seaver the top-paid athlete in Mets history. (Gene Kappock/NY Daily News Archive); (Above) Tom Seaver accepts the 1969 Cy Young Award from Jack Land, secretary treasurer of the Baseball Writers Association of America. (Dan Farrell/NY Daily News Archive)

Friday, September 4, 2020

JOHNNY BENCH REMEMBERS HIS FRIEND AND TEAMMATE TOM SEAVER

"He was just an exceptional human being"

by Bill Madden

Johnny Bench was rummaging through his closet on Wednesday, looking for a pen to sign pictures he was going to have framed, when he came upon a Cincinnati Reds jersey from 1981 personally inscribed to him by Tom Seaver.

Earlier in the day, he'd gotten the news that his "best bud" former Reds teammate and fellow Hall of Famer had passed away in Calistoga, Calif., after a long siege of dementia and suddenly, looking at the uniform, a flood of memories flashed before his eyes. He'd forgotten the uniform was even there and now, here it was, and Bench, who'd been numb most of the day, broke down.

"It was from just one of the games he pitched to me that season," Bench said by phone Thursday. "I'd been thinking about him all day and here's this uniform, signed by Tom, and he's with me again. I just lost it."

They were Hall of Fame batterymates with the Reds from 1977 — when Seaver was traded over to Cincinnati after an acrimonious contract dispute with Mets

Tom Seaver is very surprised as Cincinnati's Johnny Bench grabs and kisses him. (Bettmann / Contributor)

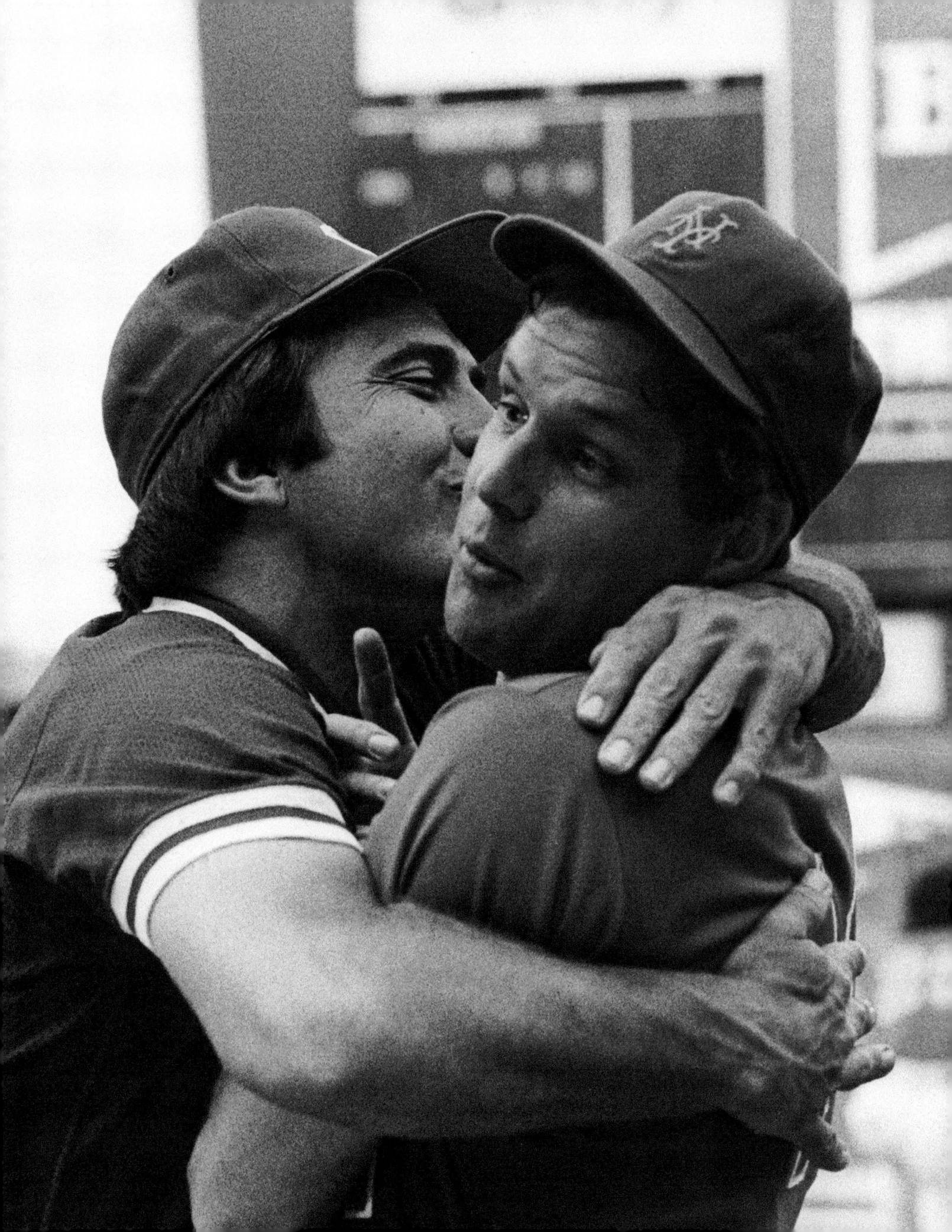

Tom Seaver has a ball noting his 20th win of the season in 1971. (Dan Farrell/NY Daily News Archive)

board chairman M. Donald Grant — until 1982 when the Mets, under the new management of Nelson Doubleday and Fred Wilpon, reacquired their franchise pitcher in a trade. During that time, Seaver won 75 games on his march to a career total of 311, including his only no-hitter, June 16, 1978, which Bench did not catch.

"He never let me hear the end of that," Bench said. "What did you ever do for me?"

But theirs was a pitcher-catcher camaraderie like no other. After they both got elected to the Hall of Fame they teamed up to transform the induction weekend by personally calling all the other Hall of Famers and imploring them to return each year. "It's baseball's high Holy Day of obligation," they told them, "you need to be here. Plus it's fun."

"I was so lucky to have had Tom Seaver in my life," Bench was saying now. "He was just an exceptional human being. I have so many memories that I'm cherishing right now."

Like the 1970 All-Star Game in Cincinnati when Seaver, coming off his signature 1969 Cy Young Award season with the Miracle Mets, was the starting pitcher for the National League and Bench was the starting catcher.

"The game started in the twilight," Bench recalled, "and after Tom threw a couple of fastballs to (Luis) Aparicio, the first batter, I called for a curveball. Tom signals to me to come out to the mound. 'No, no, no' he screams at me. 'We're throwing nothing but fastballs tonight. In case you haven't noticed, it's twilight, they can't see a damn thing.'" He was right, of course. Seaver threw three shutout innings, striking out five, including Aparicio leading off the game.

It was the same thing, Bench said, when Seaver retired from baseball and started up his own winery in Calistoga.

"I'd call him and tell him I'd really like to buy a case of his wine," Bench said, "and ask him what kind of a discount he'd give me as his fellow Hall of Famer. 'No, no, no,' he says. 'No discounts.' So I said: 'What if I buy two cases?' 'No, no, no' he says. 'We don't do discounts here, John.' And then he says 'Call my niece,' (Karen) Seaver who was the business manager of the winery. 'She'll take care of you.'"

Bench said he'd been getting calls all day from friends asking him about Seaver and what it was like to be teammates with one of the greatest pitchers of all time. "I tell them: 'If you knew him, no words are necessary, and if you didn't know him, no words are adequate,'" Bench said.

Even though it had been more than a year since Bench had talked to Seaver, not a day had gone by that he didn't think about his friend. He privately grieved for this true intellectual having been afflicted with dementia.

"I am not going to grieve any longer," Bench said. "I am going to celebrate the fact that I had him in my life."

Tom Seaver trades his ball and glove for a baseball bat in front of Mets fans. (NY Daily News Archive)

TOM SEAVER | 1944–2020

Juliette and Charles Seaver chat with Charles's brother, Tom Seaver, at Charles's East Ninth Street pad in 1971. (Gene Kappock/NY Daily News Archive)

Terrific | **DAILY NEWS**

Wednesday, September 2, 2020

TOM SEAVER, THE FIRST ONE WHO MADE METS FANS BELIEVE, WAS THE ACE OF NEW YORK

by Mike Lupica

There have been other great baseball pitchers and there will be other pitchers. Just not here, and not the way Tom Seaver was a great for the Mets once. They called him "The Franchise" and that is exactly what he was, in lights, because more than anyone, he was the Mets.

He was the one, more than anyone, who brought National League baseball back to New York. The Dodgers were gone from Ebbets Field 10 years by the time Seaver came to the Mets. The Giants were gone from the Polo Grounds. I have written this before about Tom Seaver: He didn't take away the pain of the Dodgers leaving Brooklyn and the Giants leaving the Polo Grounds. But once the ball was in his right hand and his right arm was coming forward at Shea Stadium and his knee was covered in dirt, it hurt a little less.

He was the Mets the way Michael Jordan was the Bulls. He didn't win the way Michael did. There was only the one magic October, one of the most magical times a team and a city and their fans ever had in baseball, when

Tom Seaver, circa 1970. (AP Photo)

Tom Seaver warms up Jets quarterback Joe Namath at Shea Stadium. (Dan Farrell/NY Daily News Archive)

the Mets finally won a pennant and then a World Series just seven years after they came into existence, and Jimmy Breslin was writing a book about them that asked "Can't Anybody Here Play this Game?" There was just one other trip for Seaver's Mets to the Series a few years later, in 1973.

But Mets fans know. Baseball New York knows. You do not measure Tom Seaver in the titles he won. It was not who he was and what he was in a Mets uniform. No Met will ever matter more. He was to young Mets fans in the '60s and '70s what Mickey Mantle had been for the Yankees when he was a kid in the 1950s. It wasn't until his seventh year in the big leagues, with the Mets on their way to that second World Series, that Tug McGraw, Tom's teammate, turned "Ya Gotta Believe" into the team's rallying cry.

But it was Seaver who first made Mets fans believe, truly. Mostly that baseball miracles were possible. He wasn't just the ace of his staff at old Shea Stadium. He was the ace of New York, on either side of town, as far back as you want to go. If you had one game you needed to win, for the old Dodgers or Giants or the Yankees or the Mets, you would have given the ball to Tom Seaver when he was young.

Tom Seaver: Gone now at the age of 75, having lived out the last years of his life never

Tom Seaver in a jubilant locker room at Shea Stadium in 1973. (Bettmann / Contributor)

TOM SEAVER | 1944–2020

Tom Seaver flashes 1969 and 1973 baseballs commemorating two of his Cy Young Awards. (Nick Sorrentino/NY Daily News Archive)

having recovered from Lyme disease and lost in the fog of dementia, leaving his memory and his memories to the rest of us.

M. Donald Grant would trade him away to the Reds, out of meanness and spite in 1977. Seaver would pitch for the Reds after that and he would win his 300th game for the White Sox, in Yankee Stadium on a Sunday afternoon. He pitched for the Red Sox in 1986, and was on the wrong side of Shea one more Amazin' night at that place, when the Mets came back to win Game 6, a couple of nights before they would win their first Series since '69.

But he was never Cincinnati or Chicago or Boston. He was Shea. He was New York. He was the Mets. It was a thrill to watch him pitch, especially when he was young, when he set out on what should have been a unanimous first-ballot selection to the Hall of Fame. But the only thing better than watching Seaver was knowing him. He was smart and funny and no matter where he did go after he left the Mets, he was always going to be the Miracle Mets of '69. No city ever had a better baseball time than that.

This is what he said the day he finally retired from baseball for good, after one last try at a comeback with the Mets in 1987:

"There are a lot of emotions in this decision; a lot of sadness. But I had a beautiful 20-year career. It was a lot of work, but it brought joy to a lot of people."

He brought a lot of joy to a lot of people. The day they closed down Shea for good, it was him and Mike Piazza, pitcher and catcher, who walked through the outfield and through the centerfield fence and closed the door. When the All-Star Game came to Citi Field in 2013, of course it was George Thomas Seaver who threw out the first pitch. I told him that night that the pitch he threw sure looked like a strike to me. Seaver laughed that high-pitched laugh of his and sounded young again and told me that my eyes were officially as bad as his arm.

He won 311 games and lost 205 and won three Cy Young Awards. He was inducted into the Hall of Fame in 1992. There is a beautiful sort of symmetry to the fact that his rookie year came right after Sandy Koufax's last year with the Dodgers. Koufax, a Brooklyn kid, started out his career with the Brooklyn Dodgers. He left when they left for Los Angeles, and had his greatest years there. But back in New York, there was this right-handed kid, a kid from California, who became the right-handed kid for the New York Mets. One Koufax. One Seaver. If a baseball team is blessed by the baseball gods, it gets one like them.

Tom Seaver was ours. He left New York far too soon. He dies much too young. This was sad news on Wednesday night. But with it also came the joy of which he once spoke. Once more last night, in our memory long after he had lost his own, it was October of '69 again, and he was young. ◾

Thursday, September 3, 2020

REMEMBERING TOM SEAVER, THE BROADCASTER

"He didn't want to be second best at anything"

by Bob Raissman

The words were part biting, part mischievous. They easily rolled off Phil Rizzuto's tongue.

"Seaver, you Huckleberry," the Scooter would often say. Seaver was off-camera so his reaction was not apparent.

They worked together in WPIX-TV's Yankees booth, which on paper didn't seem right. Rizzuto, the off the wall legendary Yankees shortstop, a diminutive dandy, an everyman hero. And Seaver, Tom Terrific, The Franchise, the Southern California Golden Boy, who carried the Mets from nowhere to a championship.

Yet Seaver's personality was more Yankee and Rizzuto's more Mets.

Seaver did not suffer fools gladly and often presented an aloof façade. Rizzuto was a man of the people, who read birthday greetings during games while also extolling the virtues of the cannolis loving fans brought to the broadcast booth.

Eventually, some of Rizzuto rubbed off on Seaver. Like in the seventh inning of a 1989 PIX Yankees game. Rizzuto, as he was known to do, had left the Stadium and was on the George Washington Bridge. Not immediately

TOM SEAVER | 1944–2020

Broadcaster and pitching instructor Tom Seaver talks with Mets manager Bobby Valentine at spring training in 1999. (AP Photo/Mark Lennihan)

Tom Seaver pitches to Reds star Pete Rose in 1975. (Dan Farrell/ NY Daily News)

TOM SEAVER | 1944–2020

"He grew exponentially over time into a very good broadcaster."

—John J. Filippelli

---

recognizing Rizzuto had split, Seaver read the 7th inning trivia question.

Obviously, there was no answer coming from the homeward bound Rizzuto.

Seaver, now fully aware of what went down, said: "I stumped you on that, didn't I."

Rizzuto was just one influence on Seaver. While still pitching for the Mets, Seaver worked playoff and World Series games from NBC and ABC, working with the likes of Vin Scully and Howard Cosell. And while he was in it, Seaver took the business of broadcasting as seriously as he took the business of baseball.

"He grew exponentially over time into a very good broadcaster," John J. Filippelli, president/production of the YES network who worked closely with Seaver when he was the coordinating producer of NBC's MLB "Game of the Week." "Tom applied the same dedication he had for baseball to broadcasting. He had a desire to learn and that served him well. He didn't want to be second best at anything."

In addition to his national work, Seaver did color commentary for both Yankees (1989-93) and Mets (1999-2005) broadcasts before giving it up to move to a vineyard in California.

Filippelli became good friends with Seaver. Although he wasn't part of the PIX crew, he would often go to Yankee Stadium to hang out and offer advice to Seaver. He saw many different sides of the legendary pitcher and explained why Seaver could be both standoffish and engaging.

"Tom hated being famous," Filippelli said. "I saw him spend 20 minutes telling someone why he wouldn't sign an autograph when he could have easily just signed in 20 seconds. That was just Tom. He felt he had to explain himself."

Filippelli paused. His voice cracked a bit. Then he regained his composure.

"Sometimes, Tom got a bad rap," Filippelli said. "But if you could crack that veneer you couldn't find a better guy in life."

Tom Seaver, circa 1976. (AP Photo)

Terrific | **DAILY NEWS**

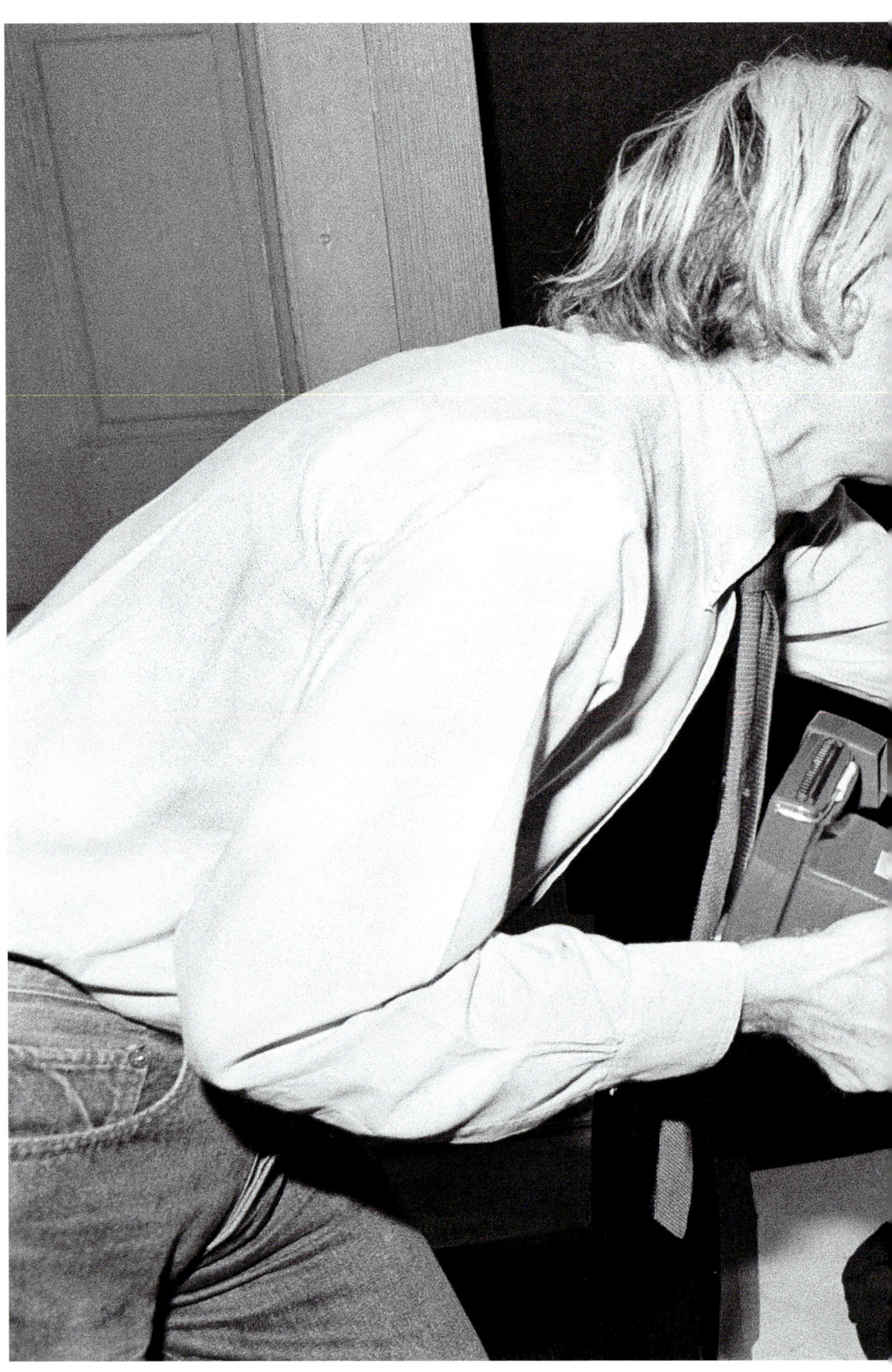

Tom Seaver poses for pop artist Andy Warhol at Warhol's New York studio, July 20, 1977. (AP Photo/Carlos Rene Perez)

TOM SEAVER | 1944–2020

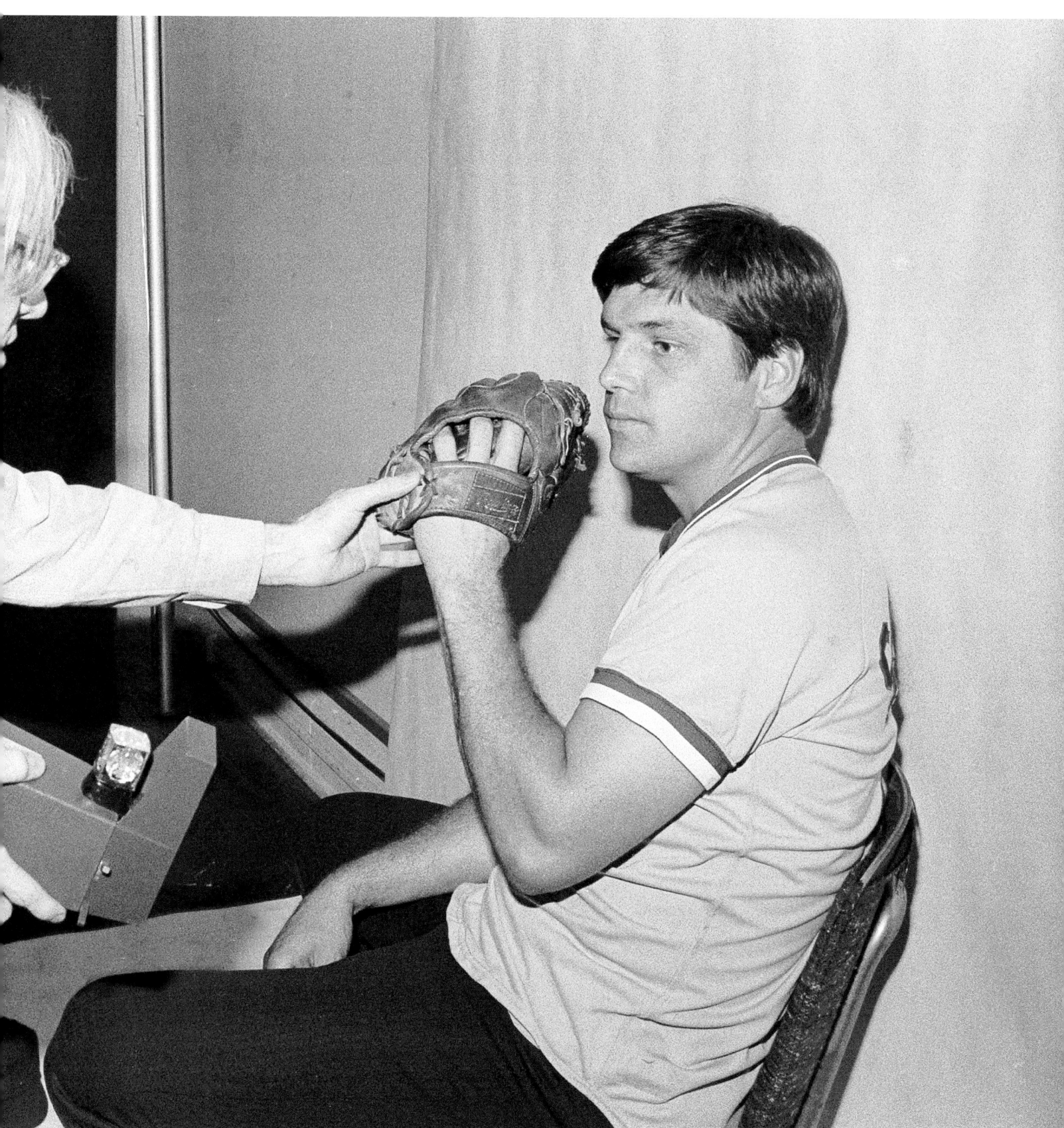

Tom Seaver and his nephew, Erick Jones, join Mets owner Joan Whitney Payson in her box before the start of Game 1 of the 1969 World Series. (Dan Farrell/NY Daily News Archive)

Tuesday, March 26, 2019

MEMORIES OF TOM TERRIFIC: HOW THE LEGEND GAVE A CHANCE TO A ROOKIE WRITER

by Malka Drucker

The announcement that Tom Seaver, the Mets' greatest pitcher and one of baseball's greats, was leaving public life because he had dementia surprised and saddened me. In 1978 I wrote my first book and his first authorized biography.

I had begun to write a book about the Mets' owner, Joan Whitney Payson, and wanted to hear from her star pitcher, "The Franchise." Playing a key role in the Mets' astonishing World Series win in 1969, Seaver was the magician of the Miracle Mets, responsible more than anyone else for taking the worst team ever and turning them into champions.

We met in an office at Shea Stadium. He put out his hand, *that* hand, exuding the charisma of a star athlete. Quickly revealing a sharp mind and quick wit, Tom spoke warmly of Payson's generosity and loyal faith in the young club. At the end of the interview, I said, "I haven't seen any children's biographies about you. Want to do one?"

He smiled and said, "Sure."

No one wanted a book about Payson. I launched my fledgling career as a children's book writer by announcing that Seaver had

Tom Seaver, Joan Whitney Payson, Art Shamsky, and Mets general manager Johnny Murphy at Toots Shor's. (NY Daily News Archive)

authorized me to write his biography. Holiday House was interested.

Tom connected me to his coach, best friends and his parents in Fresno, where he grew up. In their house there was a family portrait of Tom at 5 with his parents and much older siblings. In his father's arms surrounded by his mother who had played basketball and his tall brother and sisters, it was obvious that Tom was the adored little brother.

Tom, however, yearned to be one of them, not a mascot. That was the determination he brought to the Mets.

At our first meeting in the L.A. Hilton restaurant where we met for breakfast, Tom wore a spiffy three-piece Sears suit without a tie, one of his endorsements. The second endorsement, Aramis, filled the room. We were both 32, yet he seemed older, perhaps weary from celebrity. Everything in his life revolved around the art of pitching, and I heard a wistfulness. At best he had 10 more years to do what he loved best.

Only now do I understand how intimate a relationship a biographer has with her subject. For a year, I got to be Tom Seaver. When his mother told me how heartbroken he was when he was too young for Little League, I identified for a different reason. It was okay for me to be a wild Giants fan like my mother, but wanting to play center field like Willie Mays wasn't. Girls watch, they don't play.

Writing about Tom wasn't the same as playing, but it was close. When I described him on the mound going into his magnificent wind-up, it was me. I stepped back from the keyboard and imitated it. I kept a baseball on my desk to transport me into a Mets #41 uniform and played women's softball for the American Legion.

When I walked around the field, I attempted the knowing, blasé expression of sportswriters I'd read and admired, while inwardly I was doing cartwheels. I confessed to Roger Angell that I was writing my first book. "Just write in your voice," he advised. I stood behind the catcher in front of a screen and watched the motion of the breaking ball over and over, almost hearing the spin on the ball blurred by its speed.

It's easier to write about baseball than physical and cognitive decline. How good that I can write a sentence today. How unfair that this has happened to a very nice man.

I hope that the winery Seaver began with all the passion and devotion he brought to baseball, and his family, hold him high and tight, as his father did long ago. If I still know him, he remains brave, grateful for his remarkable life, and honest about his long day's journey into night.

Abundant thanks, Tom Terrific, for taking a chance on a rookie.

Drucker is the author of "Tom Seaver: Portrait of a Pitcher."

Tom Seaver throws against the Philadelphia Phillies on Opening Day in 1983. (AP Photo/Richard Drew)

TOM SEAVER | 1944–2020

TOM SEAVER | 1944–2020

Sunday, March 17, 2019

WHEN GOD WAS A METS FAN: HOW THE MIRACLE IN '69 HAPPENED

by Jacqueline Cutler

It was a season of dreams.

One summer, half-a-century ago, Americans walked on the moon. Half-a-million hippies turned an upstate New York farm into a festival. And a team of lovable losers somehow transformed into legends.

How was any of it even possible?

Tom Seaver had an explanation for the last one, at least.

"God is living in New York," he explained. "And he's a Mets fan."

Mostly, though, this is an upbeat success story, one that began for the Mets in 1968, with the arrival of manager Gil Hodges. The team had been cellar-dwellers since their start in 1962. But, Hodges immediately announced, "We're not going to be the same old Mets."

They had been assembling an excellent team for some time. The unflappable Tom Seaver. The spirited Jerry Koosman. Solid players like Ron Swoboda, Tug McGraw, Ed Kranepool, Cleon Jones and a young Nolan Ryan. Even the beloved Yogi Berra was there, as part of the coaching staff.

Part of the entertainment, too, as his prime job seemed to be sending players away scratching their heads. Yogi's best piece of

Tom Seaver pitched a near-perfect game against the Chicago Cubs in 1969, allowing only one hit. (Walter Kelleher/ NY Daily News Archive)

> "God is living in New York.
> And he's a Mets fan."
>
> —Tom Seaver

batting wisdom? "If you can't hit it, don't swing at it."

If the Mets loved to laugh, though, Hodges didn't share their sense of humor — especially when they ended '68 in next-to-last place.

"Losing isn't funny," Hodges announced when they returned for spring training in '69. "It's a sickness." He told them they made dumb mistakes, and that they had to try harder. But then he told them something they hadn't heard before: "You're better than you think you are."

It took a while for those words to sink in. But at the end of May, the team started an 11-game winning streak. By early September, they were on fire. The Cubs remained serious rivals, though, and a critical two-game showdown loomed at Shea.

The Mets had momentum. The Cubs had crusty manager Leo Durocher, fond of snarling, "Nice guys finish last." Even winning wasn't enough for Durocher. You had to rub the other guy's nose in it a bit, too. Show him who's boss.

If he thought that was going to intimidate the Mets, he didn't know them.

At the bottom of the first, Cubs pitcher Bill Hands knocked down Mets leadoff hitter Tommie Agee with a high-and-fast one aimed just under his chin.

Koosman watched and nodded.

And when it was his time to take the mound, Koosman fired a ball so hard at Cubs slugger Ron Santo that Santo flew backward, nursing a hurt wrist.

"You mess with my hitters, I'm going after your best one," Koosman said later. "I'll go after him twice, if I have to!"

The Mets won that game, 3-2.

During the next game, a black cat mysteriously appeared on the field and stared right at Durocher before slinking off. You didn't need to be a superstitious ballplayer to interpret that omen.

The Mets won, 7-1.

The team clinched first place in the NL East on Sept. 24, a perfect double play letting them take out St. Louis, 6-0. Thousands of

A black cat famously passed by the Chicago Cubs dugout during the 1969 pennant race. The Mets won the game and eventually the National League championship and the World Series. (John Duprey/NY Daily News Archive)

TOM SEAVER | 1944–2020

fans rushed the field, while the players rushed to the clubhouse. They still had to make it through the playoffs, facing the mighty Atlanta Braves.

Those games were somewhere north of nerve-racking, especially when Seaver gave up eight hits, including a homer by Hank Aaron. The Mets still won, and Aaron put his fist through a window but returned the next day, stitched-up and ticked-off. The Mets won again. And then again.

Fans stormed the field, tearing up everything they could find. Now only the

(Above) Tom Seaver and Yogi Berra tell the world the Mets are No. 1. (Vincent Riehl/NY Daily News Archive); (Facing page) October 10, 1969, "Reach!", New York Mets. (Bill Gallo/NY Daily News Archive)

"REACH!" —By Bill Gallo

Series — and the Baltimore Orioles — remained.

The Orioles seemed to have it all, great pitchers, terrific fielders, and had won the Series three years before. Only one man on the Mets roster had ever even played in a Fall Classic.

Sportswriters predicted a blowout.

It seemed possible. In the first inning of the first game, Seaver threw a blistering fastball — and leadoff hitter Don Buford somehow slammed it for a home run. "You ain't seen nothing yet," Buford bragged. Though the Orioles took that game, 4-1, the loss focused the Mets the way Leo Durocher's bad attitude had.

Baseball greats Satchel Paige and Dizzy Dean share a moment with Tom Seaver in 1969. (AP Photo)

No one was more determined than Koosman. After all, if Don Larsen could throw a no-hitter in the World Series, why couldn't he? Koosman finally gave up a hit in the seventh, but the Mets still won 2-1.

After two games in Baltimore, the team returned to Shea — for the first World Series that stadium had ever seen.

It started terrifically, with pitcher Gary Gentry throwing a perfect first inning, and then Agee homering off young Orioles pitcher Jim Palmer. Later, Agee would make two nearly impossible catches, helping the Mets win, 5-0.

The next day it was Swoboda's turn to make the catch of the day, diving to grab a Brooks Robinson liner just before it hit the ground. "Easily the play of the game," Shamsky writes, "and likely the entire World Series." The Mets won again, 2-1.

The stakes were now huge for Game Five. If the Mets won, they took the series. If they lost, they headed to enemy territory in Maryland.

It looked terrible early on, as the Orioles hit two homers off Koosman to take a 3-0 lead. There was a controversy in the sixth, as a pitch hit Cleon Jones in the foot. Or did it? Jones was awarded first base when umpires saw telltale shoe polish on the ball, and when Donn Clendenon came up and hit a homer, the Mets were back in the game.

A game they finally took when the Orioles' Davey Johnson hit one of Koosman's fastballs — and Jones made the catch for the final out.

When Jones dropped to one knee afterward, it seemed only right: 5-3, Mets. Their prayers had been answered.

They were No. 1, after pulling off one of the greatest upsets in Series history. They became the princes of the city.

"Two days later, we all appeared on the weekly Sunday night broadcast of 'The Ed Sullivan Show' to sing 'You've Gotta Have Heart,' the inspiring song from the Broadway play 'Damn Yankees,'" Shamsky writes. "It was an appropriate choice, considering the lyrics are all about overcoming great odds. But there was just one problem. Following rehearsals, most of us went next door to a Chinese restaurant and drank mai tais. 'We were all hammered,' Rocky recalled. 'Sullivan came out and said, "Oh my God! These guys can't go on – they're all drunk!" We still went on, but they had to bring a choir to sing behind us — out of sight."

All spring and summer there will be commemorations of the moon landing, Woodstock and the Mets. We mourn many from the 1969 team who died, including Gil Hodges at only 47 in 1972, and, Seaver is fading.

But that glorious and unlikely season should be remembered then celebrated 11 days before the season starts.

Thursday, June 16, 1977

SEAVER TO REDS AND KING TO PADRES

by Jack Lang

ATLANTA — Tom Seaver, the heart and soul of the Mets for the last 11 years, was traded to the Cincinnati Reds last night. The Mets received infielder Doug Flynn, pitcher Pat Zachry and minor league outfielders Steve Henderson and Dan Norman.

In another blockbuster deal, the Mets traded outfielder Dave Kingman to San Diego for left-hander Paul Siebert and utility infielder Bobby Valentine. Henderson will replace Dave as the Mets' regular left fielder.

The Mets concluded their housecleaning with an eleventh-hour deal, sending sub shortstop Mike Phillips to St. Louis for outfielder Joel Youngblood.

The announcement of the Seaver deal was made here and in Cincinnati. While Seaver went home to Greenwich, Conn., the Mets were hopeful that Flynn, Zachry and Henderson will report to Shea Stadium for tonight's game against the Houston Astros. Norman, 22, who had stolen 32 bases at Indianapolis, will report to the Mets Tidewater farm club. Norman, like Henderson, is black.

Seaver, 32 and considered the best pitcher in baseball today, won 189 games and lost 110 for the Mets in the little more than 10 seasons he was with them. He has a 7-3 record this season, having won his last three.

Only last week Seaver passed the great Sandy Koufax on the all-time strikeout list and received a standing ovation from the Shea Stadium fans.

An emotional Tom Seaver says goodbye to New York after being traded to the Cincinnati Reds in 1977. (Bettman / Contributor)

Terrific | DAILY●NEWS

TOM SEAVER | 1944–2020

Only he had fallen into disfavor with M. Donald Grant, the Mets' chairman of the board, and was branded an ingrate and a troublemaker.

Despite denials that he ever wanted to trade Seaver, Grant did in fact initiate talks with the Dodgers to exchange Tom Terrific for Don Sutton in the spring of 1976, when Seaver was unsigned.

In recent weeks the two headstrong individuals were at loggerheads, constantly airing their differences.

A month ago Seaver branded Grant a "bleeping maniac" when Grant expressed his desire to win the Mayor's Trophy game with the Yankees. Seaver apologized the next day.

But their differences remained broad and Grant ordered McDonald to make the best possible deal for the pitcher.

As a five-and-10-year player who must approve of any deal the club tried to make for him, Seaver was in a strong bargaining position. He would not go to just any club.

So on May 29 in Philadelphia, McDonald went to Seaver and asked him which clubs he would be willing to join.

"The Reds, Pirates, Dodgers or Phils," Seaver told him.

After getting feelers from all clubs, the Mets decided that the Reds' offer was the best and last night — after a day of rumors — they traded the best pitcher in baseball to the defending world champions.

In exchange, the Mets received Henderson, a minor league outfielder batting .335 in 47 games with Indianapolis; Zachry, a right-handed starter and the National League's co-Rookie of the Year in '76 who currently has a 3-7 record and a 5.04 ERA, and Flynn, a super-sub of the Phil Linz type who has a .250 average.

Cincinnati managed to make the deal without giving up a single frontline player and is now rated strong favorites to

Tom Seaver pitches against the New York Mets, circa 1979. (Focus on Sport/Getty Images)

overtake the Los Angeles Dodgers, current front-runners in the NL West.

Seaver, who pitched his last game for the Mets last Sunday and beat the Astros, 3-1, will make his first appearance in a Cincinnati uniform tomorrow night in Montreal.

The Mets expect to take a tremendous beating in the press and on radio and TV for trading the most popular pitcher in the league. But they are prepared to do so.

"We have tried to accommodate Tom Seaver," M. Donald Grant said, "but he has told us he is unhappy with the Mets and has asked us to trade him."

Grant revealed Tuesday night that Seaver, who is in the middle year of a three-year, $225,000 contract, had asked the club to renegotiate his pact.

After meeting with his board of directors, Grant advised Seaver the club would not renegotiate. Seaver then asked the Mets to make the best deal possible.

News that Seaver would be traded brought a flood of phone calls from irate fans to the Shea Stadium switchboard the last three days. Every available hand in the Mets' front office was kept busy answering the calls.

Throughout all of yesterday, Grant and McDonald remained virtually incommunicado to the press.

But the News learned they were on the phone constantly with the Reds, with Joe Torre and even with Seaver.

At exactly what time last night the deal was consummated was not ascertained. Both parties claimed it was not made until after their games. In that way, all players involved remained eligible to play.

Tom Seaver delivers a pitch during a game in 1979. (Rich Pilling/MLB Photos)

TOM SEAVER | 1944–2020

TOM SEAVER | 1944–2020

Monday, August 5, 1985

AN OLD FRIEND COMES HOME AND THRILLS US

by Mike Lupica

And so on the day that he took his proper place in history, in a most proper setting called New York City, Tom Seaver still was something splendid to see on a summer afternoon. It was Yankee Stadium, not Shea, and it was the White Sox for whom he was pitching and not the Mets. He is 40 years old and not the miracle boy from the summer of '69. But for three shining, emotional hours yesterday, Tom Seaver said to a New York crowd, "This is who I am. This is who I have always been."

And the crowd at Yankee Stadium that became his fully by the end, whose cheers built as afternoon became twilight and finally blew across toward the empty ballpark in Flushing that was his once, too, said to Tom Seaver with those cheers, "Hello, old friend." Years do not harm this sort of romance. Years do not damage greatness such as Seaver's. At 6:11 p.m. on the fourth of August in 1985, baseball's 300 Club received a most honored guest.

The ceremony seemed more special because of New York. Again: Hello, old friend. He grabbed the 300th by the throat and he was a Seaver with whom New York was well-acquainted. He gave the Yankees six hits. He

Tom Seaver reacts after securing his 300th career victory, at Yankee Stadium on August 4, 1985. (AP Photo/Forrest Anderson)

> "I knew we would get some runs somewhere. My job has always been to keep my team close."
>
> —Tom Seaver

struck out seven. He went the distance. The White Sox won, 4-1. Tom Seaver is 300-189 lifetime. Tom Seaver has gone the whole remarkable distance from the April day in 1967 when he beat the Cubs, 6-1, and won the first, and the glory road to yesterday began.

Feeling sick to his stomach

"The emotions today were like the first time I pitched in the big leagues," Seaver said in the interview room afterward. He talked about feeling sick to his stomach all day, carrying a bucket of nerves he thought he'd deposited in the past. Then he laughed. "I'm glad I don't feel this way every time out anymore," Seaver said.

Someone wanted to know when the nerves left him for good.

"When Reid Nichols (left fielder) caught the ball," he said. He was talking about the last out of the game, the one that got him into The Club.

He threw his first pitch at 3:11 in the afternoon, after an interminable ceremony honoring Phil Rizzuto that nearly became a telethon. And for the next three hours, this was a game like so many for Seaver across his career. He was like a plodding club fighter, throwing his punches inning after inning, picking his spots, giving up a run in the third, waiting for his team to get him runs. Remember that Seaver's teams are right there at .500 for his 19 seasons; triumph has never come easy. He has always been better than his teams. There has been a lot of scuffling, a lot of waiting. There have been a lot of days when he was on the wrong side of 1-0.

"I knew we would get some runs somewhere," he said. "My job has always been to keep my team close." Tom Terrific has always been real good at hope. And keeping his team close.

Then the White Sox got four runs in the sixth. The table had been set for history. Seaver could smell the 15th round. Then the whole ceremony became riveting at Yankee Stadium, in New York, as the crowd rose again and again and cheered a familiar and

Tom Seaver jumps into the arms of catcher Carlton Fisk after victory No. 300. (AP Photo/Ray Stubblebine)

TOM SEAVER | 1944–2020

Terrific | **DAILY NEWS**

TOM SEAVER | 1944–2020

noble efficiency. He ran the table with three fly balls in the seventh, from Ron Hassey and Willie Randolph and Mike Pagliarulo. Six more outs to 300. In the eighth there were runners at first and third and David Winfield came to the plate.

Strikes out Winfield to end the 8th

"You're never almost there with two runners on and Dave Winfield at the plate," said Seaver.

He struck out Winfield. Another standing ovation. The Mets fans at Yankee Stadium understood the noise. Now they had been united with the enemy. The Stadium rooted for Seaver now. Three outs to go.

"I've got some beautiful memories in New York," Seaver said. "I gave New York some great thrills, and today they reciprocated. They know what I've done over 19 years."

The Stadium said, "Go get three hundred, old friend."

The ninth. A screaming single from Dan Pasqua off the wall in right. Looked like a home run coming off the bat. Harold Baines held Pasqua to a single. Seaver got Hassey for the seventh strikeout on a 2-2 pitch. Randolph sent one deep to right, like something out of an air rifle. Baines ran and leaped and made a breathtaking catch

Tom Seaver acknowledges the ovation from Yankee Stadium fans after he returned to New York to notch victory No. 300. (Harry Hamburg/NY Daily News Archive)

against the wall; so Baines had his assist for history. Two outs. The Stadium sounded like Shea when the planes are taking off, banking over the old ballpark. And Seaver walked Pagliarulo. Pitching coach (and acting manager; Tony La Russa had been thrown out of the game) Dave Duncan came to the mound, along with catcher Carlton Fisk. Pinch-hitter Don Baylor was getting ready to step into the box.

Duncan: "It's up to you."

Seaver, to Fisk: "What do you think?"

Fisk: "You've got good stuff. You can get him."

Seaver: "Let's go."

Seaver, later in the interview room: "If you can't get up for the one out that's going to get you 300, then you ain't never gonna get up."

He brought the right arm – baseball treasure for all times now – forward with the "top to bottom" motion that has been his glorious trademark. One last time, he tried "to keep the ball active in the hitting zone." He did. Baylor lofted the ball high to left.

Ceremony became a block party

Halfway between the mound and the first-base line, Seaver watched, hands on knees. Reid Nichols caught the ball. Shortstop Ozzie Guillen did a Mary Lou Retton vault in short center. It was over. No. 300. The ceremony of the 300th became a New York block party. And Fisk was grabbing Tom Seaver and lifting him into the air, to collide with the cheers. To find the marvelous sounds of an old romance.

Then Seaver was kissing his wife, Nancy, and daughters, all of them crying their way into a rugby scrum. He embraced his 74-year-old father Charles (Seaver: "I couldn't have him flying all over the country at his age, waiting for me to get 300"). Fisk came over and got in on it, and Guillen. Then Seaver was taking his cap off and smiling his kid's smile and showing the same old mop of hair and the scoreboard said something about 300 and the cheers and the noise, pushed by memory, just kept washing over him.

"A day I'll remember the rest of my life," Tom Seaver would say later.

New York will remember, because New York has never forgotten him, or the genius, or the magic. The 300th had to be in New York. Had to be. The circle had to be completed here, the one that began on April 20, 1967.

Sport does not often get homecoming such as this. But then, sport is allotted just so many Seavers. He gave us one more afternoon of grace.

Congratulations, old friend.

TOM SEAVER | 1944–2020

Tom Seaver being interviewed after his 300th career victory. (Ronald C. Modra/Getty Images)

TOM SEAVER | 1944–2020

Monday, April 13, 2020

TOM TERRIFIC'S DECORATED MAJOR LEAGUE JOURNEY BEGAN 53 YEARS AGO TODAY

by Deesha Thosar

April 13, 1967 was a brisk and cloudy day in Flushing, Queens. The Mets were coming off five consecutive losing seasons and had just lost their Opening Day battle against the Pirates. For the second game of the season, with a paltry sum of 5,005 fans in attendance, then-Mets manager Wes Westrum decided a new face was ready for prime time at Shea Stadium.

That afternoon, there was reasonably no way that Tom Seaver — an enthusiastic 22-year-old from Fresno, Calif. — would know that 53 years from the day he made his major-league debut, and we suspect for many years after, he'd be known as "The Franchise."

Seaver held the Pirates to two earned runs, six hits and four walks and struck out eight batters over 5.1 innings that day. He opened the game by giving up a double to right field to leadoff hitter Matty Alou, two-time All-Star and uncle to current Mets manager Luis Rojas. Seaver escaped damage in the first when he struck out future teammate Donn Clendenon to end the inning.

The rookie starter received some run support when second baseman Jerry Buchek

Tom Seaver, circa 1967. (Bettmann / Contributor)

crushed a two-run home run off Bucs southpaw Woodie Fryman. But Seaver gave both runs back on RBI singles to Roberto Clemente and Maury Wills. Mets skipper Westrum let his young right-hander work out of a few jams before pulling him in the sixth after Seaver hit Alou with a pitch. Reliever Chuck Estrada wound up getting the win for the Mets that day.

Seaver's MLB debut was hardly perfect, but he gave fans a glimpse of his swing-and-miss stuff. He quickly signaled that greatness — and eventually Cooperstown — was just around the corner.

Seaver, now 75 years old, didn't waste time pitching his name into baseball history. At the end of the 1967 season, his 16 wins, 18 complete games, 170 strikeouts and 2.76 ERA set new records for the club. He garnered 11 of 20 first-place votes for National League Rookie of the Year. Seaver became the first Met to win Rookie of the Year honors since the franchise's inception in '62.

Two years after his big-league debut, Seaver would win the first of his three Cy Young awards. But 1969 was special for a different reason. Even though Seaver was the star of the Mets '69 championship team, he and many other teammates would go on to say then-manager Gil Hodges was the reason the Mets went all the way. Seaver went 25-7 that year, leading the majors in wins, and leading the Mets to their first-ever pennant win — after seven straight seasons of the club finishing last or second-to-last in the National League.

Dubbed "Tom Terrific" by fans, Seaver pitched for the Mets from 1967 to '77 — plus a one-year stint in the summer of '83. He won 311 games and struck out

Tom Seaver pitches against the Chicago Cubs in 1967. (AP Photo)

TOM SEAVER | 1944–2020

3,640 batters across his 20-year career before retiring after the '86 season. He played for the Cincinnati Reds, Chicago White Sox and Boston Red Sox and received 12 All-Star nods. In '92, Seaver was elected into the Hall of Fame with 98.8% of the vote — a near-unanimous decision.

Mets ace Jacob deGrom, with back-to-back Cy Young awards under his belt, is vying to reach Seaver's rather untouchable class of pitching. DeGrom won't match Tom Terrific's wins, but he's a World Series ring and perhaps another Cy Young award away from asking Seaver to move over and make some room in Mets immortality.

"Blind people come to the park just to listen to him pitch," Hall of Famer Reggie Jackson once famously said about Seaver. Jackson batted .226 (7-for-31) with a lifetime OPS of .932 against him, so it's obvious why the two-time World Series winner sang Seaver's praises.

But Jackson's words rang true even in 2019, when thousands of fans filled the seats of Citi Field to celebrate the 50th anniversary of the 1969 championship team. Seaver, who was diagnosed with dementia and retired from public life last March, did not attend the ceremony. But his presence was felt and his lore was honored by the Mets that day.

The Franchise. A moniker like that is designed to outlast generations of Mets fans and Seaver's name, plus everything he personified, will be remembered for many decades to come. ■

Nancy Seaver waves as her husband, Tom, leaves for classes at the University of Southern California in 1967. (Bettmann / Contributor)

TOM SEAVER | 1944–2020

Tuesday, June 23, 1987

SEAVER'S RETIREMENT BITTERSWEET

by Jack Lang

Frank Cashen referred to it as a "sad/happy day." For Tom Seaver, it was sad albeit a lot happier than his last two farewell addresses at Shea Stadium. This time the decision to leave was his own and it came only after Seaver realized "there were no more pitches in this 42-year-old arm that were competitive."

"I would have loved to help this team win another world's championship," Seaver said at his retirement press conference yesterday, "but when I realized I couldn't do a thing to help them, I didn't want to create a logjam if they had to go out and get another pitcher."

Admires powerhouse

"I think this Mets team is fully capable of winning another world's championship. A pitcher complains that he never gets enough runs. This team will score some points."

Seaver's regret, after 20 years of an incredible number of one-run defeats, is that he could not have pitched for this team.

"But this is a young man's game and to compete on that level, I just did not feel I could do it," Seaver said.

"There are a lot of emotions in this decision; a lot of sadness. But I had a beautiful 20-year career. It was a lot of work but it brought joy to a lot of people."

Seaver said that he is walking away from $750,000 with this decision.

"I have been getting paid since the 15th of the month and I could have continued to get paid — right up until Sept. 29 if I wanted.

Tom Seaver acknowledges the crowd after throwing out the first pitch before the New York Mets took on the Los Angeles Dodgers in spring training in 1999. (Keith Torrie/NY Daily News Archive)

"But this was a 'good faith' contract and when I realized I couldn't do it, I decided not to go any further. I set high goals for myself and it would have been unfair to me and to everyone in that clubhouse to create a logjam."

Seaver felt that had he had the benefit of spring training, "I might be pitching for the Yankees right now."

Nancy Seaver, who was at her husband's side, said of Tom's decision, "His mind is free and clear now to go on with the rest of his life. He no longer will have any doubts."

The Mets and Yankees were the only clubs Seaver was interested in pitching for once the Boston Red Sox (for whom he was 5-7 last year) did not renew his contract at the same terms.

"The Yankees called me in January and asked me if I was interested in pitching for them. I said I was," Seaver said. "But two days later they called me back and said they weren't interested."

Seaver thus became a victim of "the system" twice. For the Yankees to sign Seaver as a free agent, they would have had to relinquish a first-round amateur draft pick and they weren't about to do that.

When the Mets lost Seaver after the 1983 season it was because they left him exposed to draft in the re-entry or compensation pool. Seaver was bitter after that departure, especially since Cashen had gone to such lengths to bring him back from five years of exile in Cincinnati.

The first departure — on June 15, 1977 — was the result of a long contract harangue with M. Donald Grant. In that instance, Seaver actually asked for a trade rather than work for Grant and the Mets.

Seaver's first farewell from the Mets was in a tearful clubhouse session. He could not complete his planned remarks. When he left again in January 1984 in a Diamond Club press conference, Seaver accused the Mets' front office of "stupidity."

But yesterday — in a press conference held in the old Jets' locker room — there was none of that and only briefly did the 42-year-old pitcher show any signs of breaking. In reciting his opening remarks, his voice choked once or twice but he managed to continue.

"I made the decision because I actually felt I was regressing rather than progressing," the pitcher said. "I knew where I should have been after pitching three times."

Seaver, who had a 311-205 career record for 20 seasons, listed his 300th victory in Yankee Stadium as a member of the White Sox as his most gratifying game "personally, and from a team standpoint, winning the 1969 World Series." ■

Tom Seaver Day at Shea Stadium in 1988. (Dan Cronin/NY Daily News Archive)

TOM SEAVER | 1944–2020

Tom Glavine smiles as Hall of Famer and fellow 300-game-winner Tom Seaver plants a kiss on his cheek during a news conference at Shea Stadium in 2007. (Linda Cataffo/NY Daily News Archive)

TOM SEAVER | 1944–2020

Monday, August 3, 1992

CHEERS HUG SEAVER

by Bill Madden

COOPERSTOWN — What is normally a quiet green pasture of some 20 acres behind the A.C.C. gymnasium was now a sea of blue Mets caps, and at the mention of anything even remotely associated with Tom Seaver, the crowd erupted in spontaneous chants: "Let's Go Mets! Let's Go Mets! Sea-ver! Sea-ver! Sea-ver!"

Many of them had camped out overnight in order to get the choicest seats on the grass behind the picket fence that separates the masses from the Hall of Fame dignitaries. On this final leg of Tom Seaver's journey to baseball immortality, his most devoted fans — thousands of them — were feeling proud to be with him.

The ceremony began at 2:30 p.m. yesterday and you could feel a restlessness among the blue caps as the preliminary speeches dragged on. It was not until an hour into the proceedings that the first of the four new Hall of Famers, Rollie Fingers, stepped to the podium to accept his plaque. The blue caps became quiet. The man of 341 saves and the most distinctive handlebar mustache this side of 1890 paid tribute to his fellow relief pitchers: "All of you who've sat in the bullpen, waited for the phone to ring and faced the pressure own a piece of this." Then he talked of his late father, the man who most influenced his life and his career.

"I was 8 years old, playing with matches in my room, and I set the whole room on fire," Fingers related. "Later that night, my father came up to my room, but instead of scolding me, he took me out to the car and drove me down to the sheriff's office where he had them put me in a jail cell. He left me there for three hours.

Tom Seaver shows off his Hall of Fame plaque in Cooperstown in 1992. (Bettmann / Contributor)

"I learned three things from that. One, it scared the hell out of me. Two, I never played with matches again. And three, I learned respect. It's ironic, though, that in my 17 years in the big leagues my job was putting out fires, not starting them."

Next up was the son of the late umpire Bill McGowan, who accepted his father's plaque. Then came Prince Hal Newhouser, the four-time 20-game winner of the '40s who thanked the Veterans Committee "for finally making this my year."

It was now 4:15 and before the imperial commissioner of baseball, Fay Vincent, could even begin reading the words on Seaver's plaque, the blue caps had taken control of the afternoon. A huge blue and white flag with the number 41 was hoisted from behind the picket fence. And then the chants began again: "Let's Go Mets! Let's Go Mets! Let's Go Mets! Sea-ver! Sea-ver! Sea-ver!"

Tom Seaver, standing off to the side in a brown suit, waiting for Vincent to complete his task of reading the plaque, was visibly moved by the waves of affection echoing throughout the huge pasture. Upon accepting the facsimile plaque, he hoisted it over his head as if to say to the blue caps: "This is for you."

And then he spoke.

He began by talking about his life-long friend, Russ Scheidt, "who grew up on the same block with me and taught me how to wear a uniform." From there he thanked his three principal catchers, Jerry Grote, Johnny Bench and Carlton Fisk. When he got around to his long-time roommate, Buddy Harrelson, who was seated in the audience, the blue caps erupted into an ovation so loud you would have thought last year at Shea never happened.

Now Seaver was getting down to the emotional part — his family. He introduced his father, then his two daughters, and finally his wife, Nancy. He had to pause for a moment before returning briefly to baseball and the late Gil Hodges.

"Gil Hodges was the most important person in my career," Seaver said. "Above all, he taught me how to be a professional. I know that God is letting him look down at me now."

The emotion of the moment was finally overtaking him and, with his voice breaking, he concluded: "And the other person who isn't here — my mom. God love her."

Later, at the press conference inside the gymnasium, Seaver confessed, "I knew I wouldn't last very long because I knew 'mom' was coming. That was my stopping point. I knew that five years ago (when she died)."

The blue caps understood. It didn't matter to them how long Seaver spoke. They just wanted to be a part of this. And as he walked off the stage with the rest of the Hall of Famers, a single sign hoisted by one of them said it all: "Thanks for the memories, Tom." ■

Tom Seaver waves to fans at Shea Stadium before throwing out the first pitch prior to Game 3 of the National League Division Series in 2000. (Keith Torrie/NY Daily News Archive)

Terrific | DAILY NEWS

TOM SEAVER | 1944–2020

After the final game at Shea Stadium in 2008, Tom Seaver collects dirt from the mound. (Corey Sipkin/NY Daily News Archive)

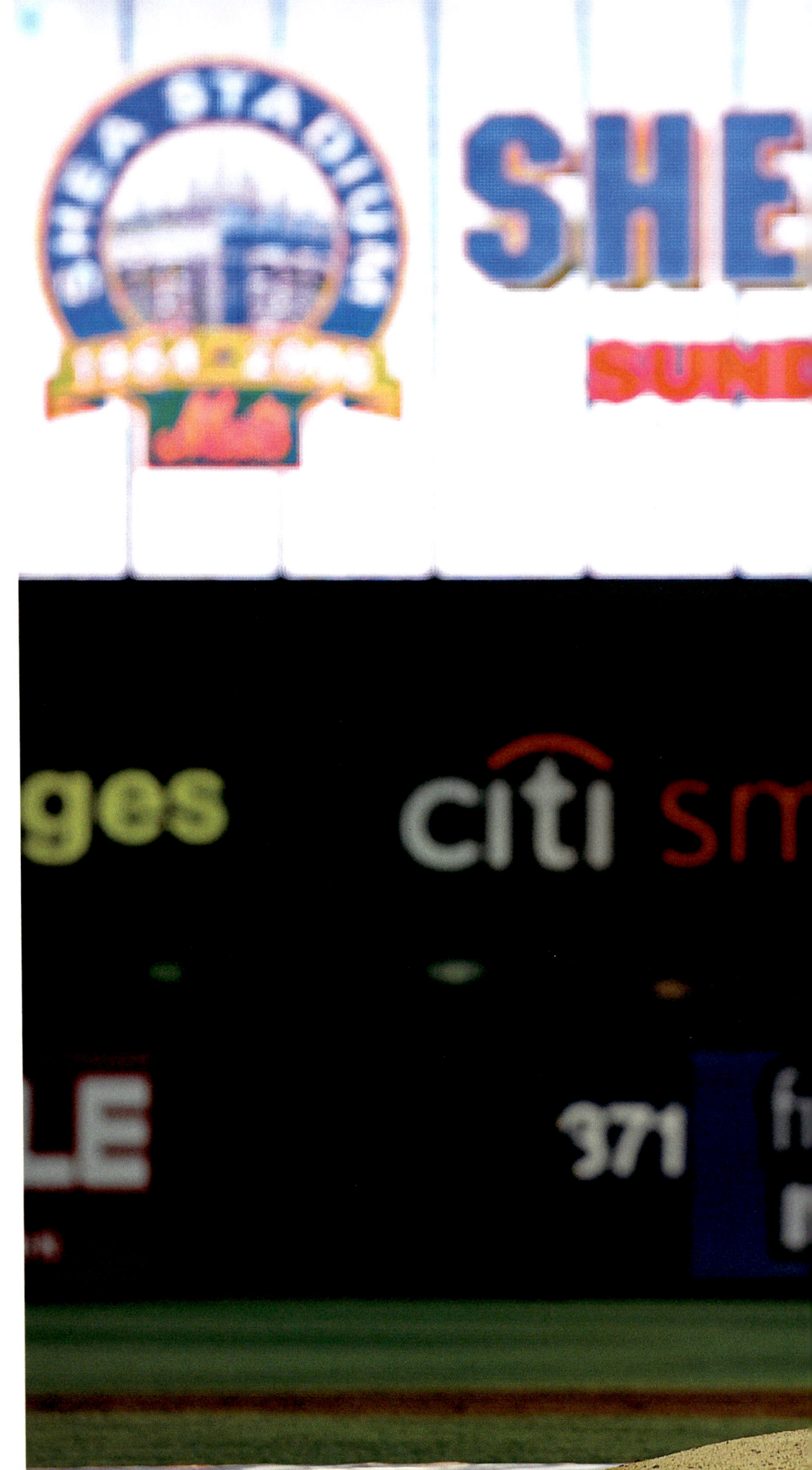

Tom Seaver walks with Mike Piazza into center field after the final game at Shea Stadium. (Corey Sipkin/NY Daily News Archive)

TOM SEAVER | 1944–2020

Thursday, March 7, 2019

TOM SEAVER'S FRIENDS CHERISH A LIFETIME OF MEMORIES WITH THE GREATEST MET

by Bill Madden

CLEARWATER, FL – From the Baseball Hall of Fame Thursday came these saddest of possible words from the family of the man simply known as "The Franchise": "Tom Seaver has recently been diagnosed with dementia. Tom will continue to work in his beloved vineyard at his California home, but has chosen to completely retire from public life."

Those of us who were close to Seaver knew this day was coming; knew the greatest of all Mets would eventually, completely surrender to the Lyme disease that had slowly ravaged his brain cells for almost a decade. The statement from the Seaver family was merely the final confirmation that we would never again see or talk with our friend.

In fact, this has been the case for nearly five months, since Seaver's cellphone shut off and his wife, Nancy – "the Queen" as he affectionately called her – also ceased all communication with his friends, the Mets, who had been hoping to somehow find a way to include him in their 50th anniversary celebration of the '69 Miracle team, and the Hall of Fame itself, where for years he reigned

Tom Seaver throws out the first pitch to Mike Piazza during Opening Day at Citi Field in 2009. (Robert Sabo/NY Daily News Archive)

as the unofficial "chairman of the board" as the Hall of Famer with the highest plurality (98.84) until Ken Griffey Jr. eclipsed it (99.32).

Speaking by phone, Johnny Bench, Seaver's closest friend, said Thursday: "I've known this was coming, we all did, but I've been content to still have those conversations in my mind with him, and look back with honor and pleasure. I know this has been terribly difficult for Nancy and the family but they had to do this because Tom was the greatest Met of all, who was loved by everyone who ever played with him and respected as a man's man by everyone in the game and anyone who was ever around him."

Still, the word "dementia" associated with Tom Seaver, the brightest, wittiest ballplayer I've ever known, is almost abhorrent. It may be dementia now, but it is really the result of the Lyme disease with which he was first diagnosed many years ago, when he was still pitching for the Mets and living in Greenwich, CT.

At the time, even though his case was severe, resulting in a temporary case of Bell's Palsy, the doctors told him there would not likely be a recurrence of it. So when he began experiencing occasional chills, headaches, memory lapses and speech problems back in 2011, he didn't associate it with Lyme disease. He thought it was just a case of a nagging flu.

Only when the memory problems worsened – one day he didn't recognize his vineyard foreman standing in his kitchen – Nancy insisted he see a doctor, where it was determined he was now suffering from Stage 3 Lyme disease. Because his friends had been concerned with his erratic behavior and glaring memory losses, they urged him to go public with his affliction.

In an exclusive interview with the *Daily News*, March 15, 2013, Seaver revealed the horrors of what the disease was doing to that great mind of his and the fear he was experiencing. "I was really scared," he said. "I didn't know what was happening. I was having trouble remembering things, making bad decisions. I said to myself: 'It's like I'm getting old before my time.' Why is this happening? I thought I'd had a stroke."

His doctors in Calistoga, CA, told him they could treat the disease with pills and medication but they could not undo the damage it had done to his brain. It would be temporarily arrested, but it would gradually progress. I visited him at the vineyard three times after that and each time his sense of humor was intact, his needling in vintage form, but his memory gradually eroding. He apologized frequently for forgetting he'd told me the same thing five minutes earlier, but we were able to laugh about it. Like Bench, I can at least still have those conversations in my mind.

"The last time I saw him at the Hall of Fame, you could see he wasn't the same," said Bench. "But then we started up on each other like always and he brightened up. 'You would've been nothing if I hadn't caught all

TOM SEAVER | 1944–2020

those pitches for you,' I said, and he laughed and laughed. And he was sharp enough to remind me I still wasn't getting any discount on his damn wine.

"I just hope because of this we will all pay more attention to Lyme disease and something good will come out of this."

The Seaver statement said he will continue to work in his vineyard every day and I hope that's true because that was where Seaver, in his private anguish, was most happy, his baseball career a long ago closed chapter in his life. I am envisioning him doing what he was doing the last time I saw him…walking the rows of grapevines in his quiet solitude, clippers in hand, with his three black Labradors – "the Rowdy boys" – trailing behind him.

Ed Kranepool, Tommie Agee, Bud Harrelson, Ed Charles, Tom Seaver, and Art Shamsky announce plans to celebrate the 30th anniversary of the Mets winning the 1969 World Series. (Thomas Monaster/NY Daily News Archive)

The video board at Citi Field displays Tom Seaver's retired number with the flag at half-staff on September 3, 2020. (Photo by Sarah Stier/Getty Images)